GO GET THAT SCHOLARSHIP!

A GUIDE TO COLLEGE BASKETBALL RECRUITING FOR HIGH SCHOOL PLAYERS, PARENTS AND SPORTS FANS

By Nate Mast

Director of Basketball Operations, Southern Illinois University

With Shawn Donnelly

ISBN-10: 1478398434
ISBN-13: 9781478398431
Library of Congress Control Number: 2012914614

Table of Contents

Two Quick Disclaimers

Disclaimer No. 1

What follows are just my personal experiences and opinions, having played or worked in college basketball for more than 10 years. Other coaches may have different experiences and opinions. You don't have to agree with everything in here. (College is all about learning to make up your own mind about things. Why not get started now?)

Disclaimer No. 2

Rules for college basketball recruiting are constantly changing. What might have been the case in some of my examples may not be the case anymore. (I may have even misremembered a few details... coaches do that). For accurate information on all the rules and regulations of college basketball recruiting and eligibility, I advise you to consult the official websites of the college-athletics organizations: ncaa.org, naia.org, njcaa.org and eligibilitycenter.org.

CHAPTER ONE

"This Is All New to Me"

"This is all new to me."

I wish I had a dollar for every time I've heard that. I would probably have a thousand bucks by now. (And I'm still in my early 30s.)

When I was head men's basketball coach at Parkland College in Champaign, Illinois, I would hear it from high school basketball players who I was recruiting. And I would hear it from their parents. They were talking about the college basketball recruiting process. Basically, they were saying, "I don't know how college basketball recruiting works. I don't know what I'm supposed to say or do here. I don't know what to expect." And it makes sense that they would say this, because it's not like there was a good manual on the subject. Which is the main reason I decided to write this thing you're reading now.

In a sense, this book is my reply to that statement. The main purpose of this book is to explain – in very simple terms – the college basketball recruiting process. To make it less new, in other words. It's written for high school players, their parents and anybody else who'd like to know more about the ins and outs of college basketball recruiting. (Like, say, high school basketball coaches. Or general sports fans. Or just really smart, beautiful, intellectually curious people.)

Anyway, by the time you finish reading this, you'll hopefully walk away with some valuable knowledge about the way college basketball recruiting works. (If you don't, I'd suggest you re-read it. This time with the TV turned off.) You'll also hopefully find it semi-entertaining. You might even laugh.

But I'm certain about one thing: by the time you read the last line of this book, you'll never again be able to honestly say of recruiting, "This is all new to me." And if someone says this in front of you, you'll be able to explain the process to them. Or better yet, hand them this book and send me ten dollars.

OK, let's get started...

CHAPTER TWO

Recruiting Is Like Dating

We'll get serious in the next chapter, but to start, it may be helpful to think about recruiting the same way you would think about dating. That's because the college basketball recruiting process is nothing more than a big singles scene, with the coaches as the suitors and the players as the pretty girls.

Don't believe me? Here are some of the parallels between the two...

Parallel #1: You're not the only one being pursued.

This is a pretty important thing to keep in mind. A lot of players lose sight of this, and it can cost them. A girl might be gorgeous and have a great personality, but at a certain point, if a guy isn't getting any positive feedback from her, he's just going to move on to another girl. Similarly, a coach may want you, but ultimately he just wants someone *like you*. Which is why, even if he's pursuing you pretty hard, you should keep in mind that he's also pursuing several other players just as hard – players who can do the same things you can do on a basketball court (more or less). So if you get interest from a coach, realize you're not the only one getting his interest. And if you get a scholarship offer, realize that it might not be sitting there on the table forever. Most coaches will have a backup plan, or several backup plans, if the first date falls through.

Parallel #2: Just because he calls doesn't mean you're going to get married.

Coaches aren't sure which high school players are going to become the best of the bunch. So they cast a wide net, invest a little bit of time and energy in a lot of high school sophomores and juniors and see which ones mature and develop to their liking. (Some even start earlier — like seventh or eighth grade.) So just because you get a letter from a coach or a phone call from a coach, that doesn't mean you're going to ultimately get a scholarship offer from him. I repeat: one letter means nothing! That same letter is being sent to probably a hundred other players just like you. That phone call? As soon as that coach gets off the phone with you, he's calling another player with a very similar skill set to yours.

Parallel #3: The only way to really lock someone up is to put a ring on their finger.

In this case, the ring is a signed letter-of-intent for a player to come play for and attend a school. Until this scholarship offer is made, a coach can make all kinds of promises, and ultimately none of it means anything. Similarly, a recruit can say whatever he wants ("Yeah, OK, I'll go to your school two years from now, Coach"), and it doesn't mean anything either. None of it means anything until there's a ring — that is, a scholarship is offered and accepted in writing. (That said, there are those kids and those coaches who do stay loyal and committed from start to finish. Those are some of the best recruiting relationships.)

Parallel #4: The long romantic weekend together is crucial.

We'll talk more about the official recruiting visit in a later chapter. But just know that it's not unlike a guy and a girl going away for the weekend, with the guy planning to pop the question to the girl at the end of the trip... assuming all goes well on the trip.

Parallel #5: Sometimes you have to speed the process up.

After your senior season, you might be invited to participate in what's called a senior showcase or an exposure camp. These are for kids who have not signed with a school yet and who want to come play basketball and be seen by coaches. And almost to a comical degree, this process is almost exactly like speed dating. There are usually three courts with games being played on them, you've got about 12 teams, the players are all numbered, and every college basketball coach in attendance has a sheet with all the players' names on it. And the kids just play, about three games each, and the coaches all walk around trying to find the player that might help their team.

And then what's also funny is you start to see groups of coaches gravitating to certain players. After a game or two, the majority of the coaches are all looking at the same half-dozen guys. It could be because they're big, it could be because they're athletic, it could be because they're making shots. But after the games are through, these half-dozen standouts are approached by each coach, who gives the kid his pitch on why his school is best. And after he has given his pitch, the coach moves on to another player and another player. So it's basically like a cross between speed dating and an episode of *The Bachelor*. It can be awkward, uncomfortable and unnatural, but at that point in the recruiting process – desperation time for both sides – it's exactly what's needed. The courtship that might take months or years happens in about five minutes.

Parallel #6: The taller ones are more attractive.

It's a simple fact: there just aren't as many good big men as there are good guards in high school basketball. So if you're a big guy (say, 6'5" or taller, 200 pounds or more), consider yourself lucky. You're going to be regarded as more valuable in the recruiting game. Don't get me wrong, guards are great, and if a coach has a chance at a Derrick Rose, he's going to do everything in his power to get him on his campus. But a big guy who can move and catch the ball and make shots is relatively rare among the high school ranks. Hence – like a stunning 5'11" woman – a talented big man turns a lot of heads.

Parallel #7: It's often important to get the approval of family members.

If you're an elite high school player, don't be surprised if a college basketball coach is charming your mother as much as he's charming you. That's because in recruiting, coaches aren't just trying to win over you, they're trying to win over anyone *related* to you. That includes Mom, Dad, best friend, girlfriend ("What would you like to study in college? Oh, wouldn't you know, our college has a great program for astrophysics!"), aunts, uncles, "uncles," cousins and other various FOFs – friends of the family.

In some cases, a coach might even recruit your teammate, because he thinks if your teammate signs, *you'll* sign. Or, a coach might recruit *you* because he actually wants to sign your teammate – or even your younger brother in a couple of years (see: Taylor and Blake Griffin at Oklahoma). Again, it's all totally acceptable behavior in recruiting. You just need to be aware of it.

Parallel #8: The more they call, the more they're interested.

Just like a guy who's calling a girl every chance he gets, if a college coach is calling or texting you every night (or every time it's legal to make the call or text), that means he's very interested. If he's not calling or texting you very often, that means he's not that interested. And if you call or text and you don't hear back from him, that means, like the book says, he's just not that into you…

Parallel #9: The popular ones are the most desirable.

If a college coach hears that you're also being recruited by three other schools in his conference, he's usually going to be interested in you. (Even if he's never seen you play.) He figures if these other schools are pursuing you, you must be a good player that he'd want to have on his team. Also, he doesn't want any of those *other* teams to get you. (Now, this isn't the way the best programs in the country do it, but you can't deny that it happens.)

Conversely, if a college coach hears that you're not being recruited by anyone else — or at least anyone else at his level — he's going to be more skeptical about your ability to help his team. (The initial thought — right or wrong — is, "If this kid isn't getting recruited by anyone, he must not be worth recruiting.") You can still change his mind by the way you play, but you'll probably have to prove yourself more than the guy who's getting attention from half a dozen schools.

That said, it's amazing how quickly a recruit can go from having no suitors to having five suitors. Coaches are copycats. Just like guys want the girl who every other guy wants, coaches want the players everyone wants. So as a recruit, you want to be coveted by as many schools as you can. That will lead to scholarship offers, and then from there you can find the right fit for you.

Parallel #10: Pictures lie.

A girl might look great on Match.com. But that might be the best picture she ever took in her life — the best angle, the best light, the best smile, the best outfit. Oh, and it was two years and 20 pounds ago. It's the same in recruiting. Through the power of editing, a lazy, inconsistent, underachieving player can look like Michael Jordan. (Or at least Marcus Jordan.) He might be playing against horrible competition. He might say he's 6'5" and he's actually 6'2". (This is especially true if he's from Europe.) He might have a terrible attitude. He might have gone 2-17 in that game, but you saw the two spectacular baskets. So as a coach, you have to verify things in person to make sure they're legitimate.

It's true from the recruit's standpoint as well. Maybe a picture on the college website shows a beautiful, sunny campus. But maybe it's actually freezing nine months a year. Maybe a jpeg from an assistant shows a gym packed with fans. But maybe that was from 1993. Maybe a highlight video shows a current NBA star playing an up-tempo style for that college. But maybe that was from a previous coach and now they walk the ball up the floor. Point being, don't believe everything you see in a picture or video. (Don't believe everything you hear, either.) Go and make sure with your own eyes. And be sure to ask a lot of questions.

CHAPTER THREE

Becoming a Scholarship-Worthy Player

OK. We've had some fun talking about how recruiting is like dating. And hopefully it helped you get a better feel for what college basketball recruiting is all about. But now it's time to take a big step back and talk about all the things you should be doing in order to *earn* a scholarship offer. In other words, now it's time to get to work. Here are actions you should be taking, starting as a freshman in high school, in order to get a college coach's attention...

Freshman Year

You've got a passion for the sport of basketball. You love watching college basketball and the NBA on TV. You love playing the game with your friends and on your school team. Maybe you've even been on a traveling team or attended basketball camps during the summer. Now you're in high school, and you're ready to raise your level of commitment.

The first thing you'll probably want to do is gauge where you're at as a basketball player. Did you make the high school team? Did you play on the freshman team? JV team? Varsity? Did you start for varsity? How good is your high school in comparison to other schools in the area? The state? Is it a 4A school that regularly makes deep runs in the state tournament? Is it a 1A school with a .500 record? The school you're at matters, because for the most part coaches recruit players from schools that regularly turn out college players. On the other hand, if you're good enough, coaches will find you no matter where you play. The thing you have to realize is this: ultimately, you'll be competing against everyone in the state (and the country) for college scholarships.

Also, you need to start figuring out what kind of player you are. How big are you? How big do you expect to be? Maybe you're 6'2" as a freshman. That's awesome. But do you expect to grow anymore? If you don't (because, say, your father or older brothers are smaller than you), then even though you're much bigger than the other kids your age, you'll still want to focus on your guard skills – for example, ball-handling and shooting from the outside.

On the other hand, if you're 5'2" as a high school freshman but your father is 6'8" or doctors have told you that you'll be 6'10" before you're finished growing, then keep that in mind. Develop guard skills – because if you're a big guy with guard skills, that will make you even more attractive (see: Kevin Durant, Dirk Nowitzski, Anthony Davis). But if you know you're going to eventually become a big man, work on your post moves as well.

If you're not sure, then develop an all-around game, inside and out. You can't go wrong if you develop the same skill set as, say, Kobe Bryant.

(Oh, and by the way, a good rule of thumb for determining height? Take the average height of your mom and dad, then add three inches. That's usually a pretty good indicator of how tall you'll be.)

Strength Training

Another thing: you should start strength training for basketball. Now, you'll notice I didn't say "lifting weights." Yes, Olympic lifts like power cleans and split squats are good, but these days, strength training for basketball is more about "functional training," which is basically training with basketball-style movements that involve a lot of medicine balls, elastic bands and explosive jumping. (The kinds of things that you see in Under Armour, Reebok and Nike commercials.)

The great thing about functional training is, you can basically start it at any age. You can find a lot of great strength training drills online – go to youtube.com/elitebasketball for some good ones. Or just go to YouTube and type in "basketball strength training." So do a little research and figure out a good workout for yourself and push yourself. (Commit to working out four days per week.) Or better yet, go in on some equipment with a friend and push each other.

And if you have the money, you might even want to hire a strength coach. (To save money, hire him for a few sessions, then replicate the sessions on your own.) Or at least try to get some advisement from someone at school who knows what they're doing. But as a general rule with strength training, go with lighter weights (or no weights) until you get the technique down, then add weight and lower your reps to gain mass.

Something else you could do: find a mentor. Maybe it's a senior at your high school. Maybe it's a former college player. Tell him that you're serious about playing basketball at a high level and see if you guys can work out together. If you don't have that kind of connection, then again, step up and educate yourself about strength training and performance training on your own. Pick up a *Men's Health*. Go to ihoops.com. YouTube "basketball drills, Duke." Pick the brains of anyone in your town/city/community/circle who knows what they're talking about and is willing to help. Maybe you've even got a younger brother or a young kid in the neighborhood who is willing to rebound for you during high-intensity shooting drills. The point is, you want to constantly be looking for ways to become a better athlete and a better basketball player. And always protect and nurture your love for the game.

Nutrition

Another thing you should be starting to do as a freshman is paying attention to your diet. Now, most kids your age won't be doing this, so you can gain a real advantage over them if you do. In general, stay away from soda and fast food. I repeat: stay away from soda and fast food. (Use the trip to McDonald's as an occasional reward, rather than a daily event.) Make sure to get vegetables, pastas, grilled chicken (not fried), fruits, milk. It may sound extreme to be focusing on your diet at this point, and I admit, I don't know a lot of kids who pay much attention to this during high school, but the ones who do will benefit from it greatly by the time they head to college. (One specific piece of advice: become a huge fan of peanut butter and jelly sandwiches. They are inexpensive and high in protein, so they're great for building muscle and adding fuel to your system throughout the day. They're also delicious.)

And of course, you definitely, definitely want to stay away from drugs and alcohol. Nothing can derail your college basketball aspirations faster than abusing alcohol or taking drugs. Stay away from the party scene, stay away from reckless personalities, never drink and drive and never get in a car with somebody who's been drinking. You can't play college basketball if you broke your femur in a car accident.

Associations

Also: this isn't really a recruiting tip, but it kind of is because we've talked about it at every place I've been. Watch your associations. Surround yourself with positive influences, people with the same goals and aspirations and work ethics as you. Keep your distance from negative people, people with no direction, no future, people who aren't going anywhere. (These people don't want to see you succeed. In many cases, they're jealous of you and want to see you end up going nowhere like them.) The positive people are going to bring out your best traits and motivate you to reach your goals. The negative people are going to bring out your worst traits and bring you down with them. They've got nothing going on in their lives, so they want you to have nothing going on in yours. Misery loves company.

So: if someone in your life isn't supporting what you're trying to achieve, drop them. You're better than that. Respect yourself. Hanging out with the right kind of people is going to make you more attractive to college coaches, I guarantee you that. They don't want to recruit a kid who they think they're going to have problems with. (One of the first questions they'll ask about you is, "Is he a good kid who makes good choices?" This includes who you hang out with.)

So start getting rid of those problems in your life now. You've got to be kind of calculated about this. Figure out, who are the kids in your class who are going places, either academically or athletically? Hang with them. Who are the kids who are supporting what you're trying to do? Hang with them. Who are the kids who, if you hang out with them, you could end up getting drunk, arrested or shot? Don't hang with them.

I don't want to get on a big lecture here, but associations are huge. There might be people who you think are your friends, and they might even have the same goals as you right now. But they're not doing so well academically. They're not making good decisions outside of the classroom. And the longer you hang out with them, the more they're not going to achieve goals and the more they're going to try to pull you away from yours so that they don't feel as bad about how they failed.

So you have to be careful about whom you associate with. I know as a freshman you're trying to make friends, but make the *right* friends. If you're going to be ambitious about basketball, be socially ambitious as well.

Team Chemistry

Now, as far as basketball, I would suggest you play with your high school team as much as you can, whether that's the 30 contact days in the summer that you have open gyms and workouts, or camps with your school. You should also be hanging out with those guys at the playground or the park or wherever you're going to play. That builds chemistry. You get to know how each other plays. You learn about each other, so when it does come time for the season, you're that much closer. That's something that gets overlooked because so many people go in so many different directions during the offseason. It's important to stay together and commit as a team to being good. Because if your high school team is good, the more college coaches will watch you. (I always compare it to this: the teams at the NCAA Final Four usually have the most guys drafted into the NBA. It's the same way for high school teams: the best ones have the most players receiving D1 scholarships. So if your team is good, you personally will receive more attention from college coaches and be viewed as more desirable. After all, coaches want winners.)

Also, the better your high school team is, the more likely it is that the better AAU teams will want you to play for them. So play together with your high school teammates. Shoot together, work out together, go to the park with each other. The more you go to the park with your high school teammates, the more motivated you will be to stay out there longer and maybe play with older, better guys – provided they're not busters who are going to try to injure you or fight you because you play for the high school team.

Another great thing you should start doing in high school is going to team basketball camps together. (A lot of colleges have team basketball camps. Look around in your area.) Also: go to other camps. Go to individual camps, go to shooting camps, go to point-guard camps, go to big-man camps. Get as much exposure as you can to different ways of playing. You'll learn from other players, get pushed by other players and coaches, and be seen by college coaches.

You could even take lessons from someone who's trusted in the community, someone who's played in college or even the pros. (Maybe they'd even take you on for free… you never know until you ask. And the worst that they can say is no, which isn't that painful to hear.)

You might think you know how to make yourself a good basketball player, but as a freshman, the more you can expose yourself to different styles and levels of play, the better. And obviously these are things you can do throughout your high school years, but if you wait too long to start, you might miss your chance. If you start bettering yourself as a freshman, you'll get to the varsity team faster, and then you'll be around better competition for three or four years rather than two. And when you go to elite camps as an underclassmen, now you actually have started what's called "recruiting yourself" – putting yourself in front of college coaches so that they can see you and your game. (We'll talk more about recruiting yourself in later chapters.)

Sophomore Year

Everything we've talked about for freshman year applies to sophomore year. You've had another year to develop, so you should have an even better idea of the kind of player you're capable of becoming. Again, you might be a 6'2" power forward now, but if you don't think you're going to get any taller, you'll probably want to start thinking of yourself as a guard. (The same goes for your junior year.) You might be that 6'3", 6'4" guy who's the tallest guy on the team, and your coach uses you as an inside guy. But you should keep working on your perimeter game because most likely you're going to need to play a wing at the next level.

So you just can't say, "Ah, I play the post. I don't really work much on the wing." Well, that's up to you. In practice, you're probably spending most of your time on the block, or setting ball screens, or scoring in the paint. But when practice is over, are you staying afterward to shoot from the outside? Are you doing some ball-handling drills? When you play with your friends, are you working on shooting from the outside and dribbling with your left hand? Of course you can take your friends in the paint because you're bigger than they are, but are you working on the things that you'll need to do at the college level? (Interesting side note: one of the reasons Dwyane Wade wasn't super highly recruited in high school was because he was a power forward, and some college coaches didn't see him succeeding at that position at the next level. Obviously, he made the adjustment to the perimeter pretty well.)

The overall point is, play as much as you can. But make it quality basketball. It's better to go full speed for 30 to 45 minutes than it is to go half-speed for two hours – or five hours. (Note: it's also okay to play two or three times a day for 30 to 45 minutes each time.) And when you're playing, work on improving your game as much as you can. Develop your skills, develop specialties, dribble with both hands, become a great shooter. Work on your pick-and-roll game, your court vision. Get stronger. Nurture your passion for the game.

Also: become a tight-knit group with your high school teammates and do everything you can with them – camps, open gyms, summer leagues. And when the contact period in the summer is over, it doesn't mean you *have* to go play AAU (where you can develop bad habits). You can still go do stuff with your high school team but without your coach – go to the park, do strength-training drills, get together and shoot with each other, run three on three, five on five.

A Few Words on AAU

An AAU team can be a great way to get you exposure. But like I said, you can also develop some bad habits playing AAU ball. Things like not guarding, shooting fast shots or bad shots, playing selfish basketball. A lot of AAU kids think they need to score 30 points and make ridiculous *SportsCenter* Top 10-style dunks to be a good player. When in reality, if no one was playing any defense, it doesn't really mean much that you scored 30 points or that you executed some crazy dunk. What's more important is that you have a grip on the fundamentals. It's not about being flashy, it's about being effective. (It doesn't matter if you made a guy look silly by crossing him over. If you miss the pull-up jumper, then you don't actually accomplish anything.)

Now, are there some good AAU teams that will allow you to play with really good players and get you exposure to college coaches? Of course. But you don't have to play AAU basketball to get a college scholarship. And some AAU teams can actually turn you into a worse player. And some guys can play themselves out of scholarships by looking terrible and sloppy on an AAU team that doesn't highlight their strengths. Basketball is about five guys being on the same page. If you're not on the same page with the four other people on the court, nobody's going to gain much. Or look very good to college coaches.

Someone might ask, "But isn't it true that most super-elite high school players play AAU?" Yes, that's true. But those super-elite players would still get recruited even if they didn't play AAU. The advantage of AAU is that it gives college coaches more of an opportunity to evaluate you. If you play in Florida, coaches from, say, UCLA aren't necessarily going to see you play during your high school season. But if you play on an AAU team that has a tournament in Las Vegas, they might see you. Bottom line: AAU is good for exposure. You're probably not going to become a better player through it.

Quick story: there was a kid from a high school near me, really good player, 6'1" shooting guard, combo guard. Played in a really disciplined, really structured system in high school. Kids played together since they were in the third grade. He was lights out in high school; the system worked for him. The coach said he was the best player he'd ever coached. A coach at a Division I school was interested in him and went out to see him play AAU. He saw a totally different type of player than the one he'd seen in high school games. The kid was playing on a team with kids he didn't play with all the time, and he just didn't play well, didn't play how the coach was hoping. After watching the kid that summer on his AAU team, the coach decided not to offer him a scholarship. So that kid essentially lost the opportunity to play at a really good D1 program by playing on that AAU team.

So just beware that AAU can actually work to your disadvantage. Because maybe that style of play doesn't fit your game, maybe your game is more disciplined. It's a little bit like Tim Duncan playing in an NBA All-Star game. He's not going to thrive in that environment. AAU is more like an NBA All-Star game than a real game.

The other message is, pick the right AAU team. Like most things in life, there are good ones and bad ones. Try to get on a good one. Try to find a coach that you like, who seems like he knows what he's talking about. It's almost the same as choosing where to play in college. You don't want to play for an AAU team with a bad coach, or with guys that aren't going to pass it, or with so many guys that you're not going to get minutes. Not that you know the answers to all of those things, but you can usually get a sense. And if it's not working out on your AAU team, it's probably best to look for a new team the next year. Keep your options open, as the saying goes.

So that's your sophomore year. You're working out with your team, you're doing strength training, you're working on your skills like shooting and post moves. You're going to camps. (If you want, you're buying elite training videos on the web, like the ones at basketballrenegades.com.) You're playing with your teammates in the park. You're playing AAU (or not). You're rising through the ranks on your high school team, from the freshman team to the junior varsity to the varsity.

Another thing I'd say is: take a good, hard look at yourself. Where does your game need to improve? Where do you need to improve, physically? You can't make yourself taller, but you can make yourself stronger. Or leaner. Or quicker. Or better conditioned.

Junior Year

Some high school players actually receive scholarship offers during their freshmen and sophomore years. If you're not in this group, one thing you can start doing after your junior season is sending stuff out to colleges – also known as "recruiting yourself." We'll dive into this process more later, but here's quickly how it works: pick out schools in the area where you'd like to play, schools where you think you *could* legitimately play. Go to their websites, find an email or a submission page, contact them, tell them you're interested in playing there. Send them a link to your two-minute highlight tape on YouTube (more on highlight tapes in a later chapter as well), and, in a brief email (two or three paragraphs), tell them your best qualities as a basketball player and as a person. Tell them your height, weight, relevant stats about your season and your team's win-loss record (if they're impressive). Something else you can do: ask your high school coach to call a college on your behalf. College coaches are more likely to return the call of a high school coach than a high school player, because even if they're not necessarily interested in you or know who you are, they know they might one day want a player at that high school.

Grades

Another way you can make yourself more attractive to college coaches is to earn good grades. In other words: compile a strong transcript. If a college coach knows you're a good student, that's one less headache for him, and one more check in your favor.

So study hard, do your homework, listen up in class. Also: by the time you're a sophomore in high school, go to your school's counselor and tell him or her that you plan to play basketball in college, and you want to make sure you take all the courses to make you eligible. You can even ask them to stay on you so that you don't slack off. Get them involved in your goal. Obviously, the better your GPA, the more attractive you're going to be to a college coach. (If nothing else, it will help you if you want to walk-on. Sometimes college coaches like to carry a lot of studious walk-ons because it raises the team's overall GPA and helps its graduation rate – two things that are becoming more and more important.)

The main thing is, you want to build up your core GPA – that is, your English classes, math classes, science classes. You also want to take a foreign language. As far as tests: take the pre-ACT and the pre-SAT as early as you can to start getting the hang of those tests and see where you are, nationally. Then in your junior year, take the ACT or the SAT (or both). Don't wait until your senior year to take them for the first time. (Note: for more information on making yourself eligible for NCAA basketball, including which core courses you need, what GPA you need and what ACT or SAT score you need, go to eligibilitycenter.org. This is also where you can register with the NCAA Clearinghouse, which you should do during your junior year, heading into your senior year. This will help you stay ahead of the game.)

Senior Year

After your senior season of high school basketball, you should try to take part in all-star games. You can legally only play in a few, but usually that's not a big concern. If you're invited to a bunch, play in the best ones. All of those types of post-season competitions – three-point contests, dunk contests – are good exposure. Or at least, they don't hurt.

Also: after January 1 of your senior year, you should fill out a financial aid form called the FAFSA (Free Application for Financial Student Aid). Go to fafsa.ed.gov and fill this out with a parent. (You'll need the tax information for the person or persons who claim you on their taxes.) It's really important that you do this in January or February, because some of the aid you can get is first-come, first-serve. The FAFSA will tell you what you qualify for in terms of grants, loans and work-study. In other words, filling it out will help determine how much money you can get during college. You should absolutely do it by March 1. The longer you wait, the more grants and scholarships you could miss out on. And you never want to miss out on free money. Assuming it's legal. And in this case, it is.

A couple final tips: start looking for scholarships outside of athletics. (This is yet another area where having good grades will help.) And if you have two or three schools you're interested in, see when you can start applying, and go ahead and apply. (But don't overdue it because most college applications cost $35 or more.)

CHAPTER FOUR

College Basketball Preparation Checklist

Here's a checklist for all of the things you could (and should) be doing during your high school years to prepare yourself for college basketball. I've separated it by basketball things and non-basketball things. Feel free to tear this out, post it on your wall, locker or refrigerator and check off actions when you complete them. (Yes, you have my permission to deface this magnificent book.)

Basketball Actions

____ Made the freshman team

____ Made the junior varsity team

____ Made the varsity team

____ Attended team camps with your varsity team

____ Attended individual camps and skills camps (shooting, ball-handling, etc.)

____ Watched videos on strength training (YouTube "elite basketball training") and/or read books about it, like *Core Performance* by Mark Verstegen and *Complete Conditioning for Basketball* by Bill Foran

____ Started a strength and conditioning program

____ Joined an AAU team (for exposure)

____ Read books about sports nutrition, like *Advanced Sports Nutrition* by Dan Benardot

____ Started a nutrition program that limits junk food and fast food

____ Started a daily ball-handling routine and shooting goal (for example, make 200 shots per day)

____ Read books on mental toughness and leadership, like *10-Minute Toughness* by Jason Selk and *The 21 Irrefutable Laws of Leadership* by John C. Maxwell

____ Read books by players and coaches you admire

____ Videotaped many of your varsity games (get the help of a friend or relative)

____ Created a two- to three-minute highlight video

____ Uploaded the highlight video to YouTube and shared it with college coaches

____ Led your varsity team deep into the state tournament

____ Reached your state's final four

____ Won the state tournament

____ Asked your high school coach to contact a few colleges on your behalf

____ Played in showcase games after your senior season

____ Visited college campuses and/or talked with college coaches

____ Played in college open gyms

____ Signed a letter-of-intent to play basketball in college

Non-Basketball Actions

____ Met with your guidance counselor your freshman year, laid out your plan to play basketball in college and enlisted his/her help to keep you on track

COLLEGE BASKETBALL PREPARATION CHECKLIST

____ Made your school's honor roll

____ Taken 16 or more core courses (like English, math and natural/physical sciences)

____ Taken four years of a foreign language

____ Taken the PLAN and/or the PSAT your sophomore year

____ Taken a class on note-taking

____ Taken a class on typing

____ Registered with the NCAA Eligibility Center (www.eligibilitycenter.org) your junior year

____ Pursued non-basketball scholarship opportunities

____ Found a mentor (someone in your family, school or community you can look up to and receive guidance from)

____ Avoided alcohol, drugs, cigarettes and chewing tobacco

____ Associated with people with similar goals and work ethics

____ Avoided the wrong people (people who aren't doing positive things with their lives)

____ Taken test-prep courses at your school and/or read test-prep books like *The Official SAT Study Guide* and *The Real ACT Prep Guide* (available at the library)

____ Registered for the SAT or ACT using the NCAA Eligibility Center code of 9999 to ensure all SAT and ACT scores are reported directly to the NCAA Eligibility Center from the testing agency (confusing, right?)

____ Taken the ACT and/or SAT your junior or senior year, earning a score of at least 85 or 1000 (verbal and math only), respectively

____ Filled out the FAFSA (fafsa.ed.gov) starting January 1 of your senior year to receive college financial aid

____ Graduated from high school with a core GPA of 3.0 or higher (you could get by with less, but come on, aim high)

____ Applied to a handful of colleges and been accepted

____ Strengthened your mind by reading books

____ Balanced basketball, academics and being a young person

CHAPTER FIVE

What Coaches Want

Every college coach is different. And yet, every college coach is the same. And sometimes you might feel like it's tough to get in his head and figure out what he's thinking, what he's looking for, what he wants. Well, allow me to take you inside. When I was the head basketball coach at a top junior college in Illinois, I looked for several things in a recruit and a player. Other coaches may look for slightly different qualities or refer to them by different names, and other coaches may value some of these qualities more than others. But in general, if you're strong in the following areas, you're going to be wanted by a lot of college coaches around the country. And more importantly, you're going to have a lot of success on the court in college.

So without further ado, here are the six traits I look for in a player. (I even had them written on a dry-erase board in my office for a while.) If you hit all of these, I want you pretty bad. And you can bet that a lot of other college coaches will, too.

1. Coachability

I want a player who is coachable. What that means is, someone who is like a sponge, ready to soak up everything the coach says and learn from everybody around him. When you look at him and tell him to do something, a coachable player listens intently, gets it right away (or, if he doesn't get it, he asks a smart question in order to get it) and then does everything he can to execute the direction. He might even throw in a, "Yes, sir."

Coachable players don't resist direction from the coach. They might question it in a way so that they can get further explanation, but it's not like they're challenging the coach. Coaches like these types of players. They're easier to deal with. They're more fun to be around. They make life easier for a coach. (A common theme throughout this book is, you want to make life easier on a coach. If you can make a coach's life easier, you're going to be attractive to him.)

So, a coachable player doesn't doubt the coach. He believes in what the coach is preaching, he "buys in," as the old cliché goes, and he is willing to do what the coaches ask him to do.

You can spot this pretty easily in games, whether a kid is coachable. If I see a kid in high school and a coach calls him over during a game and tells him something, and that kid argues with the coach or makes an excuse back to the coach or launches into a mini-debate with the coach, I'm not too psyched about recruiting that kid. You want to see a kid who runs over to the coach, gets the direction from the coach and then goes out and executes it. You want Buddy from *Hoosiers*, basically. (Toward the end of the movie, not the beginning of the movie.)

Mostly, being coachable is not the actions that you're taking, it's the reactions that you have when something is altered or doesn't go right. A coach makes a change. Do you adjust and pick up on it, or do you fight it? Do you listen to your coach? Do you show respect for your coach?

This is important because, during a season, we're going to want you to learn things and progress. If we show you how to do something in November, and in January you still don't know how to do it, then we're going to have problems. You're not going to be very successful, and neither is the team. Guys have to accept coaching, not be thin-skinned, not take it personally, not think that they're already perfect players and they can't get better. They have to be eager to get better. A coachable player does what the coach says. He doesn't have to act like a drone or a robot or anything, but he understands that the coach is the coach and the player is the player.

It can be as simple as this: let's say I go to a workout with a high school kid, and we're running a drill where you're supposed to shot-fake near the three-point line and then drive for a lay-up. And after a couple of times through, I tell the kid to try to get to the rim in one dribble rather than two. Well, the next time he does the drill, if he still takes two dribbles – if he still performs the same incorrect way after direction – then he's saying to me, "I'm not very coachable." It may not be that he's deliberately disobeying me. He might just not be paying attention. But either way, I probably don't want that guy. Because a coach has to have guys who follow directions.

2. Disciplined Background

All of these traits are kind of connected. The reason a kid isn't coachable might be because he doesn't come from a disciplined background. If you come from a disciplined background, then you're going to be respectful and disciplined with me, and you're probably going to be more coachable.

Now, what do I mean by disciplined background? I'm not saying he has to have spent the last 10 years at a military academy. But I want to see that the kid's home life has some discipline, some hierarchy. Doesn't matter if he has two parents or one or who he lives with, but there needs to be a person in his life (a parent, grandparent, aunt, uncle or guardian) who is clearly the boss, and whom he obeys. He can't run things, in other words. If the kid won't listen to Mom or talks back to Dad or just doesn't have any rules at all and does whatever the heck he wants, he's probably not going to want to come in and listen to me right away.

And I can see this when I'm recruiting someone. Mostly on the recruiting visit, but I can also pick up on this at the games, when I talk to the kid afterwards. Usually a parent is there, and how they interact is very revealing. If he's telling his mom to shut up, that's a red flag. So if you're getting recruited by a coach, be sure to show respect to your parents in front of him. That goes a long way.

There's a famous story among coaches about John Wooden, the legendary coach at UCLA who won 10 national championships. One night Coach Wooden and an assistant coach went to a top recruit's house for dinner, and Coach Wooden had the scholarship offer in his pocket. Throughout the dinner, the recruit's mother would say something a little silly, and the recruit would tell his mom to shut up. Or he'd shake his head and say, "That's stupid." At the end of the night, Wooden and his assistant coach said goodbye to the recruit and his family. On the way to the car, the assistant reminded Wooden that he forgot to give the recruit the scholarship offer. Wooden said, "No, I changed my mind. I didn't like the way he talked to his mom."

Wooden realized that if a kid didn't respect his mom, he wasn't going to respect Wooden either. Now, most coaches don't have the luxury of being as picky as Wooden was, but the same principles apply. Coaches look for kids whose parent or parents have some sort of standards, who have a set of ground rules, who have limits and boundaries. Maybe they made him work – although most of these kids don't seem to have ever had a job before they come to college – but they're definitely involved in the kid's life and he respects them.

At the other end of the spectrum, I don't want a kid who is overly babied and pampered by Mom and Dad, so that when he gets here he has no life skills or ability to take care of himself. If every problem that comes along Mom and Dad fixed, they're not going to be able to solve anything themselves, and those are the ones who end up struggling with discipline and think they are getting treated unfairly. Those are also the ones who are usually soft, mentally and physically, on the court. I don't want those guys either. I want a kid who can come into a structured system and learn to be a good teammate. If he's only acted as an individual, he probably won't be able to do that.

So basically, I want a kid in the middle. I'll take a city kid with a single parent but whose mom is on his rear end, and he has got to be home at a certain time and that sort of thing. Or I'll take a kid from a family that's relatively wealthy, but they still made their son work. Ideally, he doesn't wear the nicest clothes, and he's got the mentality that you take nothing for granted and you're not entitled to anything. You've got to earn it. Those are the kinds of kids that coaches like.

And again, you can demonstrate all of this when you're being recruited. On a recruiting visit, definitely. But even if a coach talks to you after a game, when your parents are around. Be respectful to your parents, your coach, your relatives, your teammates. And whatever you do, don't tell your mom to be quiet. (Unless she's still yelling at the ref about a call he missed in the third quarter.)

3. Basketball IQ

If you have a high basketball IQ, then you have a good understanding of the game of basketball. And in all honesty, this is probably the hardest trait to find. Because a kid may be athletic, a kid may be able to shoot, a kid might be a blur up and down the court, but can he make a play? Can he read the defense? Can he adjust? You don't have to be a basketball genius, but you have to demonstrate that you see what's evolving on the court.

There are different ways to show basketball IQ. You might be a guard who knows how to drive it, force help and kick it. (Because you realize that if a second defender has to come guard you, a teammate's going to be open.) Or you might be a guy who can catch it in the post and know that if a trap comes, you need to pass it back out so your teammate can switch it to the weak side to find an open man. Or you might just be a point guard who looks over at the bench so the coach can give him a play, and then he makes sure the team runs it. Or at the end of a quarter or a half, maybe you pull the ball back out and hold for one shot. You understand time and score – the context of the game. All of those things demonstrate basketball IQ. And that's so important, because it tells a coach you're going to be able to make the transition to a college-level game.

A guy with a really high basketball IQ can tell when a team switches defenses from man-to-man to zone. He sees danger before it happens, knows when he can slip in to take a charge. Knows when to rotate on defense, sees what the offensive guy is getting ready to do and takes it away. He has a knack for being in the right place. He knows how to foul a guy hard to prevent a momentum-swinging dunk but not make it so obvious that he gets called for an intentional foul. These are the types of plays that can secure wins. All season long. So it's a really valuable skill. And it's something that's difficult to teach, so as a coach, you really want to find guys who already have it. Looking for a role model in this area? Watch Chris Paul.

4. Toughness

Along with basketball IQ and coachability, a coach also wants to glimpse some toughness in a kid. There's a lot to be said for this. Different plays demonstrate toughness: diving after loose balls, getting to 50-50 balls first, rotating across and taking a charge on a much bigger guy, throwing your body around. A ball is going out of bounds. Does a guy watch it go out or does he jump into a crowd to save it? That kind of stuff goes a long way for me because I know that he is fearless. And if I see he *doesn't* go for balls like that, it's a big turn-off. Makes me not want to recruit him. So show coaches that you're tough.

Also, guys who are tough tend to have other good qualities, too. They're usually willing to work harder and endure more pain. Which leads to having a high motor and flying around the court. Tough guys are also usually good leaders – either by example or by showing some emotion and getting their team fired up, so that their teammates never go into a game with any fear. To me that's toughness too because you're setting an example and getting your teammates to play tougher as well, which is a big thing.

Something else: if you're tough, you're not scared of contact with opponents. You know, it's the fearless, Manu Ginobili attitude. You drive the ball and a big guy is there. Do you go in strong, take a bump and finish? Or do you wimp out and throw up a hurried air ball? That's probably the one trait that coaches see most often that they think they can fix – "I will teach that kid to finish with contact" – but it's hard. A coach can get the pad out in practice and work on it, but if a kid is soft, he is usually soft for life and he is probably not going to change too much. But either way, he has got to do it and like it.

Toughness is more easily identifiable than, say, basketball IQ. One of my players at Parkland showed me he had toughness with one play in a high school game that I saw. He was playing the 7-footer who would go on to Illinois, Meyers Leonard, and at a key point in the game, my guy, 6'2", drove into the lane and Leonard was waiting for him. Most guys probably would have thought Leonard was going to block their shot, but my guy led with his elbow and went up and hit Leonard first and still got the foul called on Leonard. I saw that, and I thought, *This kid is fearless. I want this kid on my team.*

(And he was great for me. He was the X-factor on the team, a consistent player that none of our opponents thought would hurt them. He was the kid that I would have guard 6'8" guys, because he knew how to battle with them, lean on them and get physical with them without getting called for fouls. And he could also guard a 5'10" point guard.)

Two other quick points on toughness: it's not just physical toughness, it's mental toughness. It's not getting flustered when your team's 18-point lead dwindles to a 5-point lead, and the crowd is going crazy. It's pulling your team together at that point and scoring a big basket to keep you up by a safe distance.

Secondly, toughness is also tied to unselfishness, because a tough player doesn't necessarily think about himself — his stats or even his body. When you dive on the floor, you're thinking of your team more than yourself.

5. Academics

As mentioned in the previous chapter, if you have good grades and good test scores, that takes a lot of stress off of a coach. Not only does he not have to worry too much about you qualifying to play, but it also shows that you're going to be smart enough to understand what a coach is trying to teach. One class I specifically focus on is geometry. I feel like if a kid is struggling in geometry, he's probably not going to be able to pick up the things we're doing on the basketball court, in terms of offense, defense, out-of-bounds plays and critical situations in the final minutes.

But it goes beyond geometry. In my experience, if guys struggle in English, reading and other math classes in high school, then college is going to be hard for them, and most likely basketball is going to be hard for them too. Because they can't learn at the rate we are trying to teach them. That's why I really scrutinize transcripts now. Where did the guys get Ds and Fs? If they were in history and chemistry, that's a problem. If the only As and Bs a guy got were in physical education and home economics, then I know he's one of those kids who just got pushed along and is not going to be prepared when he gets here.

You might think you don't have to worry about grades as much if you're planning to go to a junior college. But it's actually quite the opposite. If you come to a junior college and you have to take developmental math, reading and English, then you're going to be a year behind coming in and won't be able to graduate, and coaches want to graduate kids. You also have to graduate in order to transfer to an NCAA school. And the minimum GPA to transfer just went up from 2.0 to 2.5. Which means it just got *more* difficult for junior-college kids – particularly junior-college kids who aren't great students – to move on to an NCAA school.

Also, if you're struggling in math, reading and English, it's more likely that you're going to be ineligible, which doesn't help you or the team. So my advice is: pay attention in class, do your homework and study. Make it a point of pride to get good grades.

Likewise, if you score a 13 on your ACT, you're not going to be attractive to most coaches. Because as I mentioned earlier: chances are, if you can't learn in school, you can't learn in basketball either. And it speaks to an overall work ethic. If you're not working in school, it sends the message that you're less likely to work on your game. And that means you're not going to be a very good player, because every player needs to work hard on his game. Talent is overrated. It's just the start. You have to build on it. (Or, as another saying in coaching goes: hard work beats talent when talent doesn't work hard.)

6. Personality

This one comes from a couple of experiences I've had recruiting a kid who really doesn't talk a whole lot when you are talking to him, doesn't really give off a lot of positive energy. You might think he is kind of nervous or shy. But usually, it turns out what you see is what you get.

In other words, that kid who is tough to communicate with when you're recruiting him... is going to be a kid who's tough to communicate with when you're coaching him. When this kid gets on campus, he's going to be Mr. Mopey, and he's going to suck the life out of a team, and he's probably going to end up getting kicked off of it because he's bringing teammates down with him. So if I start recruiting a kid, and the first time I introduce myself and talk to him, if we can't have a conversation, I am probably done recruiting him. If it's really awkward and it's hard to get him to say stuff, or if he really just doesn't have it socially, that's how he's going to be on our team and it's going to be tough to coach him. And it's going to be tough for the team to build chemistry.

So as a high school recruit, you can make yourself a lot more attractive to coaches if you are easy to communicate with. Again, you can see why "yes sir/ no sir" guys are a coach's dream. A coach wants positive people on his team, guys who are going to support each other. You don't want a team full of really quiet dudes. That just doesn't work. If I like to be around you, then the team is going to like you. And that will lead to good team chemistry, which is huge. So be positive, be talkative, look coaches in the eye, smile, use full sentences. That will send a message to a coach that you're the right type of player for his team.

This is probably another parallel to dating, but personality goes a long way. I would like a kid who calls me and says what's up, or texts me and says did you see that game last night? If a player smiles a lot, that stuff is contagious. Pretty soon the whole team is smiling. That's why one of the things I like in a highlight video is when a kid starts it off by showing a little personality at the beginning – introduces himself, says who he is and where he's from, sounds upbeat and smiles. I'm telling you, coaches respond to that stuff. They're people too. They want to win. But they also don't want to spend four years with Debbie Downer.

A Few Words on "Talent"

You'll notice that "talent" is not one of the six categories for me. That's because talent is not only tough to quantify, it's also overrated. Was Kobe

Bryant born with talent? Absolutely. But he's not in the NBA because of that talent, he's in the NBA because of what he *did* with that talent. He's worked on his game and improved steadily from the time he was a teenager. If you're reading this, you're playing high school basketball, so you're probably somewhat talented. The question is, what are you going to do with it? How are you going to develop it? How are you going to improve every day, every month, every year? That's why, if I were going to add a seventh category, it would be: *specialty*. Develop a specialty. Get really good at one thing. You could become a great shooter. You could become a great passer. You could become a great rebounder. A great catch-and-finish guy. A great on-ball defender. In most cases, to play in college basketball these days, you need to be really good at something. At least one thing. If you're really good in one area, it's harder for a coach to take you off the court.

And if I were to add an *eighth* category, I'd say work ethic. Hard work is a skill. Some guys just don't even know how to work hard. The key is to practice so hard that the games are the easy part. So coaches want guys who are going to be willing to work hard. Who do everything the right way. Who go 100 percent. That's one of the hardest things to get guys to do – to keep the intensity level and effort level high every day, when you've got kids thinking, "Oh, I'm tired... I got this paper due... I've got this problem with my girlfriend... I don't know what I'm doing tonight..." Coaches want guys who are going to play as hard as they can play. In practice as well as the games.

And hard work gets back to toughness – mental toughness. You have to make yourself play through the pain of being tired, of your muscles aching, of being out of breath. Tough guys are going to keep working even when they're fatigued. It's like the legendary long-distance runner Steve Prefontaine used to say to his opponents, "Let's see which one of us is willing to endure more pain today."

Summary

The bottom line is: coaches want tough kids who want to play basketball and be coached. They don't necessarily want the so-called elite talented guys who don't want to listen and think they already know everything about the game of basketball. Are there exceptions to this? Sure. But most coaches are looking for these same sorts of qualities, more or less. Just recently, I was talking to one of the top assistants at SMU, and he told me, "Nate, I don't even mess with these kids if they're not tough and if they don't respect me and their parents."

So remember that. It's not just about talent. There are all these other categories that coaches desire. And you want to be as strong in as many of them as you can be. Because your well-roundedness is going to separate you from guys who may be equally or more talented, but don't have their you-know-what together.

CHAPTER SIX

The Levels of College Basketball

OK, you know what it takes to be a scholarship-worthy player, and you know what coaches are looking for. Now, before going any further, let's take a *quick* look at all the different levels of college basketball where you could end up playing.

NCAA Division I

At the top end, this is the highest level of college basketball. The one you see on ESPN. The one with the recognizable coaches and the Final Four. Earning a scholarship to an NCAA Division I school means you're a really good basketball player – or at least, you have demonstrated the potential to become one.

The thing to realize here is that not all D1 basketball programs are created equally. Although it's the division with the Final Four and the recognizable coaches, it's also the division with about 200 schools that are almost never on national TV and that you might never have heard of – schools like Wagner College and Coppin State. That's because there are more than 340 Division I basketball teams. (That's right: 3-4-0.)

D1 basketball schools can offer full athletic scholarships. That includes tuition, fees, room, meals, books, everything. (Interestingly, D1 schools *can't* offer partial athletic scholarships.) If it's a big Division I school, you'll also get plenty of shoes and gear, you'll stay in nice hotels on the road, and you'll fly to some of your games. In other words, it's big-time college basketball. You'll play in front of anywhere from a few thousand people to 30,000 screaming fans. You'll have a chance to compete in the Big Dance, get praised by Dick Vitale and Jay Bilas and be featured in "One Shining Moment." All that fun stuff. This is the level you've probably dreamed about. (And the level a million other guys have dreamed about as well.)

One other thing about D1: if you go on a recruiting visit to a D1 school, you can be offered a scholarship and you can give a verbal commitment to that scholarship, but you can't sign a letter-of-intent while you're there. You can't sign a letter-of-intent in the presence of a D1 college coach, period. (This rule exists to prevent coaches from handing a kid a letter-of-intent and saying, "Hey, sign right now or I'm signing another kid tomorrow" or anything like that.)

NCAA Division II

This is the second tier of NCAA basketball. In general, it gets a lot less media attention and fewer fans than D1. But it's still a very high level of basketball. The size and athleticism of the players typically takes a drop from D1 – although a good D2 school will often have transfers from D1 who have eligibility issues or just didn't make it at their D1 school for one reason or another.

D2 schools can offer full athletic scholarships *or* partial athletic scholarships. So, a coach might offer a recruit a .8 scholarship, which will pay for tuition, fees, apartment and books, but not meals. Or he might offer a recruit a .1 scholarship – say, just books.

D2 schools still produce the occasional NBA player. For example, both Ben Wallace and Charles Oakley played at D2 Virginia Union.

NCAA Division III

The third tier of NCAA basketball. The size, athleticism and skill level drops even more. That said, there are still some pretty good Division III teams and players out there. For example, former Laker Devean George played Division III basketball at Augsburg College in Minnesota. And to go way back, seven-time NBA All-Star Jack Sikma played at D3 Illinois Wesleyan.

D3 schools cannot provide any athletic scholarships. However, they can provide academic scholarships, and if a coach likes you, he will usually work with you and his college's financial aid office to try to get you as much academic scholarship money as he can. So D3 schools are mostly looking for really smart kids, who can either afford to pay for college themselves or who are so academically strong that they can earn an academic scholarship.

NJCAA Division I

NJCAA is the athletic association for junior colleges – also known as JUCOs. Junior colleges are two-year schools. A lot of players start at a JUCO because they don't qualify academically to go straight from high school to a four-year school (like an NCAA Division I school). These players can then transfer to an NCAA school or an NAIA school. (Note: every year at a JUCO costs you a year of NCAA eligibility. And you have a total of four years of NCAA eligibility.)

Of course, JUCOs aren't *just* an option for players who don't qualify academically to play NCAA basketball. Some JUCO kids are strong academically, but they choose to play at a two-year school to keep their recruiting options open because they didn't get the NCAA offer they desired. (For example, they might have received some NCAA D2 scholarship offers coming out of high school, but they think after a year or two in junior college, they can earn an NCAA D1 offer.)

The highest level of JUCO is Division I. D1 JUCOs can offer full athletic scholarships (tuition, fees, room, meals and books). Interestingly, a recruit can sign a letter-of-intent to play at a junior college, but then sign a letter-of-intent at an NCAA school, thereby canceling out the JUCO letter-of-intent.

NJCAA Division II

This is the second level of JUCO. D2 JUCOs cannot offer full athletic scholarships. They can offer only to pay for tuition, fees and books. That said, there are a lot of really strong D2 JUCOs. Many D2 JUCOs could beat a lot of D1 JUCOs.

NJCAA Division III

The third level of JUCO. D3 JUCOs cannot offer athletic scholarships. So if you go there, you are either paying your own way or you're getting an academic scholarship.

Some D3 JUCOs are pretty good. And just like D1 and D2 JUCOs, some D3 JUCOs have dorms and cafeterias, and some don't. (If they don't, you'll typically live in an apartment complex near the school.)

As a whole, JUCOs have produced hundreds, if not thousands, of players who go on to play NCAA and then pro basketball. A few that come to mind right away: Shawn Marion, Jamaal Tinsley and Dennis Rodman.

NAIA Division I and Division II

NAIA is just another college athletic association, with similar (but in some cases, more lenient) rules than the NCAA. Somewhat surprisingly, the NAIA includes nearly 300 smaller colleges and universities across the U.S. (and even a few in Canada). They have names like Oklahoma Baptist, Shawnee State, Oregon Tech and West Virginia Tech.

NAIA can be a good option if your "clock" with the NCAA – the amount of time you have to complete your NCAA career, after starting it – has expired. They're also good if you've already been to a couple of NCAA schools – or if you were recently released from prison. (Kidding! Kind of.) But yeah, NAIA can be a little bit of the Wild Wild West, with guys who are 28 or 29 years old running up and down the court. I applaud those guys for keeping their dream alive, though.

(And I might be exaggerating a bit on the age thing. NAIA schools get a lot of kids who might not be good enough to go NCAA D1 or D2 but want to experience a four-year environment instead of going JUCO. The scholarship is just as good and the venue could be better than most JUCOs.)

Prep School

Prep school is increasingly becoming a great option for players who don't qualify academically to play NCAA hoops after high school. In the past, these guys would go to junior college for a couple of years, then transfer to an NCAA school for their final two years. Now, a lot of them go to prep school for a year, get their core GPA and test scores up, then transfer to a four-year school. This way, they don't lose a year of college eligibility. Which is a huge advantage over junior colleges, especially for major D1 prospects.

Prep schools are also a good option for those high school players who could use another year to develop physically – and develop their game – before facing the 21- and 22-year-old "men" of college basketball.

But there are some drawbacks to prep schools. One, they can be expensive. And two, their seasons can suddenly shut down, either because the schools on their schedule don't have enough players or money to continue, or because that school itself doesn't have enough players or money to continue. Like so many things, there are good prep schools and there are bad prep schools. If you're thinking of going the prep-school route, look for one that has a history of sending players to NCAA D1 schools.

CHAPTER SEVEN

Marketing 101: The Edit Tape

Let's review. You're playing varsity basketball for your high school, and you're starting to make plays that are getting people's attention. You know what it takes to be a scholarship-worthy player, you know what coaches are looking for, and you've got an idea of the various levels of college basketball where you might want to play. Now it's time to start thinking about getting your name and your game out there – in other words, marketing yourself. Probably the most effective, most important way to accomplish that is by producing an excellent edit tape. Which can also be referred to as a "highlight tape," "highlight reel" or "highlight video." But I still call it an edit tape.

Now, when I was a head college coach, I got sent a lot of these, and I'll be honest with you. Most of them were bad. But that's good news for you, because if you can produce one that's not terrible, you're going to separate yourself from the masses. So here are some things you should definitely be sure to do when you're putting together your edit tape. Follow these guidelines, and you'll have a highlight reel better than almost anybody else in your area. (Assuming, of course, you're actually making plays for your team.)

Keep It Short

Three minutes is the ideal length. You definitely don't want to go more than five minutes. Make it two minutes and coaches will love you. The thing you have to understand is: coaches are busy. They don't have time to watch an hour-long replay of every layup you've ever made, or every practice shot you've ever taken. So respect your audience's time and keep it short. With edit tapes, like with most things in life, less is more.

Grab the Viewer's Attention

Ideally, the first five plays of your edit tape should be the five best plays of your career. Don't save them for a grand finale at the 30-minute mark. A lot of coaches, if they don't see anything impressive in the first five plays, are going to shut off the tape. So start off with a bang. Remember, you want to dazzle the coach. You want to get him excited about you as a player. You want to make his mouth water. Think of this almost as a movie trailer for yourself. In other industries, videos like this are called "sizzle reels." That's because they're supposed to sizzle. But you also have to bring the steak...

Show College-Level Plays

You want to fill your edit tape with a variety of college-level plays. What are college-level plays? Plays that would work at the college level. Plays that aren't just working because you're in high school, playing against inferior talent. So it's not just that you made a three-pointer, it's how you made a three-pointer. It's not just that you finished at the basket, it's how you finished. Here are some examples of college-level plays:

- Hustling back on a fast break and blocking someone's shot.
- Stepping out to stop a point guard on a pick-and-roll and stealing the ball and going down and laying it in (or tomahawk dunking it).
- Catching a pass in the lane and finishing with your right and left hand.
- Finishing with contact.

- Diving for a loose ball, collecting it and passing it to a teammate.
- Pulling up in transition, rising and hitting a 15-foot jump shot.
- Taking a charge on a fast break.
- Speeding past an opponent in transition and laying it up (with your right and left hand).
- Coming off a screen, catching a pass, rising up and hitting a three-pointer. Even better? Doing so from different parts of the court.
- Catching a pass at the three-point line, shot-faking, taking one dribble and hitting a 15-footer.
- Passing into the post, relocating, catching a pass and hitting a three-pointer.
- Using your body to get position in the post, catching a pass, taking one dribble and finishing. Right and left hand.
- Guarding a ball handler, sliding your feet, keeping him in front of you and earning a five-second call. Or a 10-second half-court violation.
- Guarding a guy in the post and blocking his shot; or "walling up" to make him shoot over you, then rebounding with authority.
- Coming over to help a teammate and blocking an opponent's shot.
- Driving into the lane, forcing help and kicking it to a teammate, who makes a three.
- Dribbling off a ball-screen and feeding your rolling big man for a lay-up.
- Setting a ball-screen and either rolling to the basket for a lay-up or stepping out and hitting a jump shot.
- Changing speeds while you're dribbling – starting slow and then blowing past a guy for a layup; or crossing a guy over and hitting a 15-foot jump shot.
- Fighting for a rebound and tipping it in; or setting yourself, going up strong and finishing.
- Jumping two or three times in a row quickly to get a rebound. (This is big. Coaches love a guy whose second jump is as fast and explosive as his first.)
- Getting a three-point play and firing up the crowd. (That stuff matters.)

Keep It Tight

Show only plays. Don't show any in-between stuff. Don't show you jogging backward and waiting for the other team to bring the ball down the court. If there's a sequence where you make a lay-up, steal the inbounds pass and hit a three, then yeah, show the whole sequence. Otherwise, cut between the plays so we don't have to watch anything that's not relevant to the thesis of this edit tape, which is: you're an awesome player who makes college-level plays.

Keep It About You

Show only plays where you figure prominently. If you make a pass to a guy who drives the lane and kicks to another guy, who hits a three-pointer, that's a fine play on your part. But don't put it in your edit tape. It just shouldn't make the cut of your best plays. For one thing, it's confusing to the viewer because we might not know which one you are. And for another thing, if you're including this, we start to think you must not have enough good plays of your own. It damages your overall credibility when you include a play that's not really about you, or not impressive.

Make It Clear Who You Are

This is probably the most important tip. Before you can do anything else, you have to make it clear who you are. So at the beginning of the tape, put a slide that has your name, your school, your height, your weight and your number. (Note: this is also a good reason to use the same number throughout your high school career, and your AAU career.)

If you want, you can even introduce yourself at the very beginning, to show the coach some of your personality. "Hi, my name is Tim Basketball, I'm a senior guard at Generic High. I'm 6'1", 180 pounds, I wear number 20, I'm really looking forward to playing basketball in college, and here's my highlight tape." Something like that, spoken with enthusiasm, to show the coach that you've got a positive attitude, and that you can speak in complete sentences. Obviously, you still need good plays on your edit tape, but a little touch like that will help a coach remember you and possibly separate you from the pack.

Don't Use Special Effects

When you use special effects, it sends the message that the plays you're making aren't impressive enough on their own, so you had to dress them up with computer tricks. So don't use them. Don't show plays in slow-motion. Don't show a play from multiple angles. Don't have any crazy swirls or starbursts or cross-fades. Just show the plays (ideally from a camera situated at midcourt at a decent elevation). If you want to show a particularly great play more than once, that's fine. But don't show it more than twice.

And to repeat: don't use slow-motion. The reason being, it usually comes off as desperate – and sometimes it's even comical. Like, I've gotten edit tapes where a guy throws the ball off an opponent's leg – and it's shown in slow-motion. When I see something like that, first I might laugh. Then I'll turn off the tape because I know this guy is a clown.

One exception to the no-special-effects rule: it can be helpful, at the beginning, to put a spot shadow on yourself for the first couple of plays so the viewer gets a feel for what you look like on the court. Again, this is good because it's not just a flashy special effect; it's actually serving a purpose – it's making you easier to see on the court.

Show Games, Not Shootarounds

Don't send coaches a video of you shooting around with your father on a side court. (Yes, I've gotten those.) Those would be terrific if coaches were assembling kids for a three-point contest, but they're not. They're trying to win games. So show plays from games. With referees. On regulation courts. Ideally, against good competition.

Don't Use Offensive Music

You don't have to set your edit tape to music, but if you do (and most kids do), just be sure not to use music that has cuss words or offensive language or anything like that. That's going to be a turn-off to coaches and send the message to people that you're a certain type of player (namely the wrong type), even if you're not. So if you want to set it to rap, fine, but don't make it explicit rap. (A coach might be watching the video at home, and his kids might be listening.) Maybe go with something more like Kanye. (Radio-friendly Kanye.) Or instrumental. Or take a cue from the international kids and go with techno. (It's always techno with the international kids. Kind of funny.)

In Terms of Editing...

These days, with digital cameras and editing software on computers, it's a lot easier to make an edit tape than it used to be. You can do it yourself, or you can ask somebody to do it for you. Here's what I would do. Acquire the digital video footage from some of your best high school games. (If you don't have this yet, get someone to start taping your games with a digital video camera. Midcourt. Decent elevation.) Upload this footage to your computer (or to a computer at your school). Use editing software on your computer to cut the footage into an edit tape like we discussed. (If you don't have editing software, there are some software programs available online that you can download for free – programs like Microsoft Movie Maker, Avid FreeDV, Wax and Apple iMovie... if you've got a Mac.) Once you've created a winning edit tape, convert this into a WMV file or upload it on YouTube or Vimeo.

The other option is to go to your team's student manager or the president of your school's A.V. club or someone else you know who is fairly tech savvy and ask them to do it for you (with your input, of course). Chances are, if you ask nicely, they'll say yes. If they're hesitant, sweeten the deal by telling them that they can give themselves an edit credit at the end. (And that you'll let them hang out with you.)

In Terms of Formatting...

In the old days, you'd create tapes or DVDs of your highlight reel and mail them to coaches. Good news: it's not that complicated or expensive anymore. You can still go the DVD route if you want, but honestly, I wouldn't even bother. Not only are they more expensive, but half the time they don't work on the coach's computer or DVD player, which is annoying. You can avoid all this by simply uploading your edit tape to YouTube or Vimeo. Or emailing it to people as a WMV file. Either of those options is really convenient for coaches, which is the key to them actually watching it.

Another tip: once you've created an edit tape that you're happy with and you've uploaded it to YouTube, tell all your friends about it so you can start getting some views. That way, when a coach sees it online, it won't have only 7 views or whatever, which will immediately make the coach think what he's about to watch must not be very impressive. As mentioned before, recruiting is like dating. To a certain extent, your popularity – or lack thereof – matters.

In Terms of Distribution...

Once you've got an edit tape you're happy with, the next step is getting it out there to coaches. Hopefully you've taken a look at a few levels of basketball, and you know where you'd like to play and where you think you *can* play. Make a list of these colleges. (It makes more sense to focus on the schools in your area, because coaches from these schools – if they like what they see in an edit tape – will actually be able to come watch you play.) Go to their websites. Find the coach's email addresses or a page on the website where high school players can submit information about themselves. (Nearly all colleges have one of these options, or both, on their websites.)

Fill out this player profile form or send the coach a short email – two to three paragraphs, max. Say who you are, what year you are, where you play, maybe list your best qualities and your stats if they're good (although coaches hardly ever pay attention to stats because they can be so misleading, depending on what division you play in), and say you're interested in playing at his school. Then, either attach the WMV file of your edit tape or include a link to your edit tape on YouTube or Vimeo ("You can see my edit tape here: link"). Leave your phone number and address at the bottom. Say thanks. Be brief and positive. Check for spelling and grammar errors before sending.*

Do this for 20-30 schools in your region. If you feel like doing it for more, go for it, but be realistic and realize that the farther you get from your home, the less likely you are to hear back from coaches. (Why? Because they know they can't come look at you in person, for one thing. The exception to this is if you play in a really talent-rich state. Then, you may get *more* interest from farther-away schools.)

You may not hear anything. Don't worry about it. Realize that coaches are busy. Keep playing basketball and working on your game. If you don't hear anything in a month, follow up with another email. And don't set your heart on one school. Cast a wide net.

If you do hear back from a coach and he asks you to send something else (like, say, a transcript), send this information as soon as you can. How you handle that simple request will tell a coach a lot about the kind of person and player you are – how diligent you are and how much you want to play college basketball. Give him everything he asks for as soon as possible.

A Few Words on Recruiting Services...

As you may know, many places offer to create edit tapes for you and promote you online – that is, send out your edit tape to "interested" college coaches. In my opinion, you don't need to use them. As I explained above, you can do it yourself or have someone from your school help you with it. But if you *do* want to get the help of a video service (purely for their access to editing equipment and their skill with producing highlight videos), I would say this: do your homework and find a video service that creates the kind of edit tapes I've described above – simple, no-nonsense high-light videos. Avoid the recruiting services that churn out edit tapes that make everyone look the same, the kind that use way too many bells and whistles and look "overproduced." If you use one of those, college coaches are going to put you in a certain category in their mind. Frankly, they'll assume you're the kind of player who isn't good enough to get attention on his own, so he needs to hire someone to make him look good.

Take Care of the No-Brainers

These things probably go without saying, but: use a decent camera. Make sure there's decent lighting. Make sure the video works once you upload it. If you're sending DVDs, make sure they work in both computers and DVD players. And as far as plays are concerned: show a variety, not just the same type over and over again. Show you can do a lot of different things on the basketball court.

In Summary...

Make it clear who you are. Let your plays shine through, not your graphics. Keep it short. Keep it tight. Keep it clean. The end result should look pretty simple. But as you'll find in life, sometimes it takes a lot of work to make things look simple.

*Here's an example of the kind of email you want to send. I received this while I was head coach at Parkland.

Dear Coach Mast,

My name is [REDACTED] and I am a basketball player from Coach [REDACTED]'s program at North [REDACTED] High School in [REDACTED], Indiana. I am interested in attending Parkland as a student and a player this fall. Here are a couple of things about my game. The best part of my game is my defensive intensity. Although I play the one or two positions, my strength, speed and overall agility allow me to defend multiple positions. In practice, I guarded Tyrone [REDACTED] (Big Ten recruit) and D'Vante [REDACTED] (top 25 player in the state). Coach credited me for their growth because I worked them so hard at practice. I also have a very versatile offensive game. I'm a good enough dribbler to bring the ball up the floor and I am a solid midrange shooter. I can post up and finish as a two or a three. A link to my edit tape is below. Please contact me. Here is my cell. Here is my dad's cell. I'd like to know when you are having workouts. Also, here is my coach's cell. Thanks for your time.

Sincerely,

[REDACTED]

I like this email because he's not just blowing smoke. It's clear he knows his role and where he could provide value to a team. It's not overly desperate. It's understated. It's respectful. (He's not saying, "Hey Coach, call me and tell me about your program" like some of the emails I received from other aspiring college players – emails I saw and thought, "Are you kidding me?") And maybe most importantly, it's not full of spelling errors. Because if you can't write me a note without a bunch of spelling and grammar errors, you're not going to be able to pass English class. So I'm not going to waste time with you.**

**Unless you're just awesome. Then, we'll get you a tutor.

CHAPTER EIGHT

Beyond the Edit Tape: What Else You Can Do

All right. You've created a killer edit tape. (It's climbing up the charts on YouTube.) You've cold-emailed some schools and coaches with it. You're in your junior or senior year of high school, putting up solid numbers and doing good things for your high school team, which is above-average in your area. And you're *still* not getting much love in the form of letters and calls from college coaches.

First of all: don't worry. You're not alone. This happens to a lot of guys (as the saying goes). But the good news is there are some other things you can do, beyond the edit tape, to market yourself and distinguish yourself from the crowd. Here are a few suggestions...

Develop a Specialty

As mentioned earlier, coaches are looking for guys who are really good at one thing. Solid in all areas, but really exceptional in one area. Could be shooting. Maybe you need to become a more consistent three-point shooter (and a more aggressive shot-taker in games). Could be rebounding. Maybe you need to focus on getting your rebounds-per-game average up in double digits. (Set goals for yourself.) Maybe it's lockdown defending and rallying your team on the defensive end, leading the conference in charges taken (if they kept that stat). Maybe it's overall leadership and toughness, throwing your body around with a bit more reckless abandon and firing up your teammates, being more vocal. Figure out what one thing you have the ability to be great at, and pursue it with a madman's intensity. Which is a good thing to have on the basketball court anyway.

Get Your Coach to Make a Few Calls

By your senior year, you should definitely make it clear to your high school coach that you want to play basketball in college. Then, toward the middle of the season, you might start asking him about his college connections – in other words, if he's friendly with any college coaches in the area. You could also just ask if he has any tips on where to start. (Few people will know your game, and where you might be able to play, better than your high school coach. And, ideally, few people will want to fight harder to find you a spot at the next level.)

Or maybe you've got your eye on one or two colleges in particular at this point (and you've watched them play and you're pretty sure you could play at their level). In that case, ask your high school coach if he could call those coaches on your behalf and speak highly of you. As previously mentioned, college coaches are *much* more likely to return the calls of high school coaches than high school players. That's because they know that even if they might not want this particular kid (or know much about him), there could come a time when they *will* want – and maybe even really, really, really want – a kid from that high school. So it's in their best interest to stay on good terms with high school coaches, and at least hear your college coach out.

By the way, that call from your high school coach could be as simple as, "Hey, College Coach X, this is High School Coach Y. Just wanted to let you know, you're going to be getting an email from High School Player Z with his information and edit tape. He's a great kid, really worked hard for me the past three seasons, and I think he'd be an excellent asset to your team, so please take a look at his email and edit tape. If you have any questions, give me a call at this number. Bye." If you provide your high school coach with the college coach's phone number (and you should), it would really only take about 60 seconds of your high school coach's time. (Something you might mention to him, if he's hesitant to follow through. And heck, you could even write up a short script for him like the one above, so he doesn't even have to think about what to say. Again, make things easier on your coaches, and they'll love you.)

Get Someone Else to Make a Call

If your high school coach isn't too keen on making any calls on your behalf – maybe he's got a mountain of American History papers to grade – see if there's another coach familiar with you (perhaps your AAU coach) who's willing. Or maybe there's someone else with some basketball credibility who can vouch for you to a college coach. Even your mom or dad could try calling. It's worth a shot. For whatever reason, a college coach is often less likely to blow off a parent than a kid.

Participate in All-Star Games and Exposure Camps

After your senior year, definitely try to play in as many all-star games and exposure camps as you can. You want to get your face and your game out there so that you put yourself on the radar of as many college coaches in the area as possible. (And when you play in these all-star games, make sure you, like, play well. Don't get too selfish, but bring your A-game and stay aggressive.) Look at these games as an opportunity to showcase your skills and also learn from your teammates. You might even find that you play better around this group of players that's more talented, and when the overall speed of play is increased. Sometimes that happens.

Keep Writing Emails and Sending Edit Tapes

The worst thing they can do is say no. Or not respond. And emails are free.

Expand Your Search

If you happen to be in a state with really good basketball, try broadening your search to include colleges outside your state, where the level of play isn't as strong. For example, you might not be considered top-tier for Illinois, but for Montana, you could be considered a blue-chip player.

Check Your Coach's Mailbox

This probably goes without saying, but at some point ask your high school coach if he's been getting any letters from colleges about you. You hear stories about coaches receiving letters for their players and throwing them out. Not sure why coaches would do that, but it's worth asking about to make sure it's not happening to you.

Send Even More Emails and Edit Tapes

If you're determined to play basketball in college, there's really no limit to how many lines you can send out. Because the more you send out to colleges, the better chance you have of at least one of them responding. It's like shots on goal in hockey – the more you shoot, the more you'll score. And as Wayne Gretzky said, you miss 100 percent of the shots you don't take.

Follow Up

If you've sent an email or made a phone call and some time has passed (a few weeks, a few months), follow up. Call again. Send another email. Ask if you can meet. Ask for a workout. Ask when they're having open gym. Ask them what their needs are, what they're looking for, how many spots they have open. Ask if they've watched your edit tape. Offer to send your edit tape again. And sell yourself. Talk about your best qualities, the things you can bring to a team. Keep knocking on the door. Be polite but persistent. Most coaches will respect the hustle, even if they find you slightly annoying.

Use a Recruiting Service

As mentioned earlier, there are services that will help you get your name out there to college coaches. Berecruited.com, for instance, is one of the bigger services. At my junior college, I got emails from them all the time telling me about players from all over the country who were (allegedly) interested in playing for me. And I usually deleted those emails immediately. Or after watching two plays on their edit tape and not seeing anything I liked. So I don't really recommend going this route. Their credibility is super super suspect because they're going to make every player sound great, even when he's not. Because that's their job; that's who's paying them.

But, if you don't mind blowing some money and you've tried everything else, feel free to use one of these services to get yourself on some more coaches' radars. I'm sure they've worked for some players.

(Note: these services probably work better for other sports, like lacrosse or soccer or hockey. I just don't think they're really an effective service for basketball, where there are so many kids playing it, the standard to get a scholarship is so much higher and there are more scouts out there analyzing kids to make sure nobody amazing falls through the cracks. Because another thing you should realize is, most college basketball programs subscribe to several credible recruiting services/websites that evaluate high school players all over the country and deliver unbiased evaluations. So if you're a great high school player, chances are you're being evaluated and written about by one of these independent recruiting services that coaches subscribe to.)

Start Thinking About Walking On Somewhere

We'll talk more about this in a future chapter. But there's no shame in walking on to a college team – that is, playing for the team without a scholarship. And there have been lots of guys who have gone from walk-ons to key contributors for college teams. Even a few NBA players were former walk-ons – guys like Jeff Hornacek and Scottie Pippen. Heck, I walked on at the University of Illinois.

Start Thinking About Being a Team Manager

It worked for Lawrence Frank. He didn't even play high school basketball, but he served as a team manager at Indiana University, then became the head coach of two different NBA teams. If your real dream is to coach basketball, maybe you don't even need to play it in college. Study up and get an academic scholarship to a school with a really good basketball program, and volunteer to be a student manager. Who knows, in 15 years, you could be making hundreds of thousands more dollars (as a college or pro coach) than most of the guys you were handing towels to.

Make a New Edit Tape

Maybe you've made better plays since your last edit tape. Maybe you've improved your edit-tape-making skills. Maybe you've got a new camera. Might be time for a new highlight reel. Tip: make this one shorter. And lose the Kenny G.

A Few Other, Crazier Options...

Move to Canada

Kidding. Kind of.

Become the Best Friend of a Five-Star Recruit

Then say it's a package deal – both of you, or neither of you.

Turn Your Phone On

Maybe you just had your phone off.

Continue Growing

Scottie Pippen was 6'1" when he entered college. He left 6'7". Maybe you just haven't gone through your growth spurt yet. Maybe your body is still a little awkward right now, but you're going to be taller and stronger and smoother when you're 19 or 20 or 21. You never know how your body is going to develop, and what kind of a player you can be when it does. So keep eating that corn and drinking that milk.

CHAPTER NINE

Coach K Is in the Building...

... or maybe it's Roy Williams. Or maybe it's the third assistant for Southeast Missouri State. In any case, when a college coach is attending a high school game in person – whether to scout you or another player – you should consider it your chance to grab him by the throat (figuratively speaking, Latrell Sprewell) and force him to notice you.

So, you ask, what's the best way to get a coach to notice you? In a lot of ways, it's by demonstrating the same qualities that you'd show in an edit tape – that is, by making college-level plays. But there are some qualities a coach can evaluate much more effectively in person. I've listed the main ones below. Demonstrate enough of these, and a coach is going to walk out of that gym thinking about you – whether or not he knew who you were when he entered it.

Catch and Shoot

If you're a shooter, a coach is going to want to see how quickly you can catch the ball, get your balance, rise up and knock down a shot. He's also going to want to see if you're constantly moving off the ball to get open (something you can't really see in an edit tape), if you're correctly reading screens, how much time and space you need to get your shot off, if you can create your own shot off the dribble, and how efficient you are as a shooter. In an edit tape, a coach only sees the makes. In person, he can see if you went 5-8 from three-point range, or 5-18. But more important than the exact numbers are the overall mechanics. Because it doesn't matter how good of a shooter you are if you can't get your shot off at the next level. Aim for the mechanics of Ray Allen or Kevin Durant and you should be okay.

Take Care of the Ball

If you're a point guard, coaches want to see that nobody ever takes your ball. You can handle tight, belly-to-belly defending, you can dissect a full-court press, you can navigate a trap. None of that fazes you, and nobody ever rips you. It's important that you demonstrate these things, because a coach really wants to be able to trust his point guard not to turn the ball over. And if you *do* turn it over, you'd better hustle like crazy to try to get it back.

The second thing is, do you run your team? Are you vocal? Are you directing traffic? Coaches want to see this from you. Thirdly, are you a good passer? Are you feeding the post really well – throwing it to your big guys where they want it, where only they can get it? Are you making sure your passes don't get deflected by the guy guarding you (by, say, pass-faking, waiting for your man to land and then feeding the post)?

You don't have to be a great scorer as a point guard to be viewed as highly valuable to college coaches. A guy like Joey Rodriguez at VCU is a great example – not a huge scorer, but the ball was safe in his hands, he ran the team, and he got his teammates involved. Any coach is going to want a guy like that.

Finish with Contact

For big guys especially, it's very important that they can take a hit and still finish. So if a coach is attending your game, you want to show that you can handle contact, that you embrace it… that you can bang. A coach wants bangers. He doesn't want a big guy who doesn't like to be touched. That limits a player and what he can do for a team. He wants a guy who initiates contact, who can take a little punishment and hand it out as well. In short, he wants a guy who doesn't back down. (It all comes back to toughness.)

Another desirable trait for big men is good hands. You can't finish with contact unless you can first catch a dish from a teammate. You don't have to be an above-the-rim guy, and you don't have to dunk. You just have to be able to catch a pass – even if it's a little off-target – and finish. Ideally with both your left and your right hand.

If you don't feel like you have very good hands – or you can't finish effectively with either hand – work on it. There are tons of drills you can do to improve your catching ability and your weaker shooting hand. (YouTube: "catching drills, basketball.")

Motor

Just like football coaches, basketball coaches talk about a player's motor. Which means: how active is he? And this is something a coach can really gauge better in person. Is the player always moving? Does he play with a lot of energy? Does he seem to be everywhere on the court? You don't have to be the best player on the floor – or even touch the ball very much – to be viewed as a "high motor guy." For example, a guy like Joakim Noah for the Bulls has a high motor. Matt Howard for Butler had an incredible motor – he was always eager to set screens, fight for rebounds (on defense *and* offense), take charges, leave his man on defense to stop a drive, sometimes guard two guys (help and recover). And the end result was that he seemed like he was everywhere. (He wasn't afraid to commit the occasional hard foul to prevent an easy layup, either.) Coaches love guys like this. Coaches love guys who race around the court and do all the dirty work. And it's much easier to *get* a guy like this than to try to *teach* a guy to play like this.

Good Teammate

What are you like in warm-ups? Are you pumping up your teammates, or are you keeping to yourself, walking around like you're too cool for this place, and yawning? Coaches want positive people on their team. They don't want "clubhouse cancers." So when coaches attend a high school game, they really watch for this stuff. During the game, are you helping up the teammate who took a charge? Are you encouraging your teammates and boosting their confidence, so that they play better? Are you listening to your coach during timeouts? Are you cheering for your teammates when you're out of the game? All of that stuff matters. If you're dissing your coach or acting like you're too good for your teammates, that's a major turnoff. A dealbreaker, even. I've seen coaches write a guy off simply by how he behaved in warm-ups.

No Terrible Weaknesses

Another dealbreaker: not being able to dribble. Or having no left hand. Or not being able to guard anybody. In other words, you can't have any terrible, glaring weaknesses. You might be a great shooter, but if you can't dribble without getting the ball stolen, a coach knows that's going to be a much bigger problem at the next level. So if you've got weaknesses in your game, identify them now and work on them – before the college coach shows up to watch you. Ideally, you should try to work on your weaknesses so much that they eventually become your strengths. Or at least not your Achilles heel. (To improve his subpar handles, for example, Jimmer Fredette used to dribble in the dark through narrow hallways. Jimmer also signed a "contract" in high school, at his older brother's urging, promising to do the work and make the necessary sacrifices to reach his ultimate goal of playing in the NBA. Which you could also do. But I digress.)

Handle Adversity

This is a huge one. Maybe the most important one of all, in terms of what coaches try to gauge when they watch a kid live. When things aren't going your way, how do you respond? Do you crumble under the pressure? Or do you stay calm, avoid getting frazzled and even take your game up a notch? For instance, when you're on the road, and your 12-point lead shrinks to a

2-point lead in the last few minutes, and the crowd is going berserk, what do you do? Do you give in and let the other team – and its crazy fans – steamroll over you? Or do you dig in, step up your defense, demand the ball on offense and make a big play for your team? Obviously, coaches want the latter.

In fact, Kansas head coach Bill Self has told me that he actually wants to see a high school kid not when he's having the best game of his life, but rather when he's having the *worst* game of his life. He wants to see how you respond when things *aren't* going your way. When you're not getting the calls, when your teammates are blowing layups, when your shots aren't falling, when your team's down by 15 and the fans are yelling expletives at you. What do you do in that moment? How do you react? Do you still play hard, still fight, still believe? Do you still play tough defense, get important rebounds and drive to the basket to get on the free-throw line? Do you wilt under the pressure, or do you grit your teeth, dig deeper and take your game to another level? How you respond to adversity is going to say a lot more about what type of player you are than what you do when you're coasting along with a 20-point lead. Bad times reveal a lot more about character than good times. That's when you really get to see what a guy is made of.

So if a coach comes to watch you play, and you start out 0-for-6 and your team's down by 15, just think, "I got the coach right where I want him."

CHAPTER TEN

A Letter Means Nothing: Handling Interest from Coaches

You walked to the mailbox one day, and there it was: a letter. From a college. Saying they're interested in you playing basketball for them.

First of all: congrats. Second of all: don't get a big head. It means nothing. If it's from a big school, they probably sent the same letter to 500 other kids across the country. (Sometimes I think it's these big-time colleges that are keeping the U.S. Postal Service in business, with all the mail they're constantly sending to potential recruits.) So, you haven't made it yet. You haven't really done anything. Don't quit your day job, as they say.

Now, should you feel good about yourself, for attracting attention from a college? Of course. But you shouldn't jump to any conclusions. This doesn't mean they're going to offer you a scholarship. This doesn't mean they "want" you. This doesn't mean they've ever even seen you play. They might have just gotten your name off of some scouting service's list. Who might have just gotten your name off someone's All-Conference list. Who might have just gotten your name off someone's preseason All-Conference list. So don't go telling your friends or posting on Facebook that you know where you'll be playing basketball in college.

Also: this doesn't mean you should shut down your recruiting, turn a blind eye to "lesser" programs, stop taking the phone calls of schools from lower NCAA divisions or junior colleges or anything like that. In other words, you should keep your recruiting wide open, which will keep your college options wide open. Basically, you should still try to get the attention of as many schools as you can.

Because again, all this program that sent a letter to you is doing is the equivalent of you telling a hundred different girls, "Hey, I'm watching you. Maybe we'll go out one day." Doesn't mean you're ever going to go out. Doesn't mean you're going to get married. These coaches are just trying to reach out to you now and make a good impression because you have the *chance* to be good, and so if you actually develop and *become* someone they want, they can say, "Hey, we've been on you since day one." If you don't develop the way they hope, they can drop their interest in you in a second and move on, and they haven't lost anything except a little bit of time and money on postage.

So what this also means is: you shouldn't stop working on your game. You shouldn't stop trying to become a better player. Don't assume, just because you got some letter from, say, Indiana, that you're necessarily good enough to star for Indiana, or even play for them. Like I said, they probably sent that same letter to hundreds of other kids. There's obviously not room for all of them on the Indiana roster. So to separate yourself from everyone else that school is recruiting, you need to stay hungry and keep trying to improve every day. Don't start settling. Don't start slacking off. Don't get complacent.

If anything, you should see that letter as a challenge to work even harder, to get even better. Think of it this way: "Oh, all they sent me was a form letter? I want to impress them enough that they'll start calling me. And then once they call me, I want to impress them enough that they'll come visit me. And then once they visit me, I want to impress them enough that they'll offer me a scholarship. And then once they offer me a scholarship, I want them fighting for me against other schools, and praying that I'll say yes to them." So don't take your foot off the gas when you receive a letter from a college. Rather, press it down even farther. Because you don't want your greatest basketball achievement to be, "I once got a generic letter from Kentucky."

Phone Calls...

The same goes if a coach starts calling you. Realize he's calling a bunch of other guys, too. I'm not saying don't get excited. I'm just saying, be yourself. (Or at least an upbeat version of yourself.) Don't think you have to start acting completely differently. Don't think he's about to offer you a scholarship over the phone, and don't say anything crazy like, "I definitely want to play at your school." You can say you're interested in finding out more about the school – that's fine. Just don't jump the gun and think there's about to be a marriage proposal here. You're both just feeling each other out. Especially if it's a first call.

If you want, you could even start looking at it as a business call. In other sports and other countries, athletes are professionals at 16 or 17. Why not start thinking about yourself as a professional? The truth is: this guy is interested in potentially acquiring your services next year. Be respectful. Be polite. Feel free to show him your personality. But don't get so awed by the process that you start acting unlike yourself, or you start agreeing to things you're not comfortable agreeing to. Be honest. Be respectful. Be outwardly humble but inwardly cocky. Say things like, "I appreciate your call... that sounds really interesting... I'd love to hear more about that..." Don't say things like: "So are you offering me a scholarship, or what?" or "I'd love to play at your school!" (But most importantly: talk! Give more than one-word answers. Show that winning personality and your ability to communicate, like we talked about earlier.)

And don't let it be a one-way street with the questions. You should be feeling out the coach as well. Ask him things you want to know about him, and the school, and the program. Things like:

- How's the team doing this year?
- What division is the team? (NCAA, JUCO, NAIA, etc.) Note: you probably wouldn't ask this of an obvious D1 program.
- How many kids go to the school? Is it a campus or a commuter school?
- How many years have you been at the school?
- How long do you plan to stay there?
- What style of basketball do you guys play?

- How do you see me fitting in? / What position do you see me playing?
- How many guys are you recruiting at my position?
- How many scholarships do you have for next year? (Or for the year you'd be coming in.)
- How many guys on the team do you have coming back at my position? (Try to get an idea of how many returners will be back.)
- If you're feeling brave: what parts of my game do you think I need to work on?
- How far away is the school from my town?
- How are the academics at the school? What are some of its best programs? (If there's a particular program that you're interested in, ask if they have it.)
- Do you guys have tutors for athletes?
- How is your strength program? / Who is your strength coach?
- Which coach would be working with me the most?

And so forth. You just want to get as much information about the coach and the team and the school as you can. And by asking these questions, you'll get a sense of how much this coach wants you (by how much time he's willing to spend talking to you, for one thing). You'll also get a sense for how excited you are about the prospect of playing there. Although, make sure you're getting excited about it for the right reasons – for example, not just the program's tradition and the uniforms, but the current coach's style of play and style of coaching, and the players who are currently there.

To say it another way: try to gauge how much a place excites you, but then try to make sure it's exciting you for the right reasons – actual, good, concrete reasons, not fantasy reasons. You want to make sure you're not ignoring some huge problems with you actually playing there. For example, if your game is running and fast breaks and theirs is walk-it-up-the-court, it's probably not a good fit for you, no matter how much you might like their school colors and uniforms.

And of course, you could probably find out answers to a lot of the above questions on your own, with a little bit of research. So some of them you might just want to look up after the first conversation. (The next time he calls, he'll definitely be impressed that you did a little homework on him and his team and his school.) But having said that, sometimes it's good to ask those questions even if you sort of know the answer, just to see how the coach answers them.

Texts and Tweets...

Increasingly, college coaches are communicating with recruits through texts and tweets. Especially now that the NCAA allows coaches to send unlimited texts and direct messages to high school players as long as they've finished their sophomore season. (The rule was changed in June 2012.) Overall, you should approach texts with a coach the same way you would a phone conversation with him. That is, be positive, be professional, be the best version of yourself, and don't be afraid to ask questions. And if there are more complicated issues that you want to discuss, feel free to ask the coach to call you. Or call him. Because as useful as texting can be for quick exchanges with someone, it's not the best medium when you've got a lot on your mind. For that, it's still better to have a live discussion – like over the phone, or face-to-face.

Also keep this in mind: for every hour you spend texting someone, that's an hour you can't spend becoming a better basketball player. So just try to be efficient with your communication, and then get back to what's important – schoolwork and basketball.

And while we're on the subject of tweets, here's what I would say about being on Twitter: be careful with it. Sure, having a Twitter account could theoretically help you garner more attention from college coaches (by demonstrating that you're intelligent and giving them a way to quickly contact you). And sure, it's kind of fun to tell everyone what TV show you're watching and what you had for breakfast.

But I think there's a greater chance that it could hurt you. Look at all the professional athletes who have gotten themselves into trouble by posting ill-advised comments on Twitter. If you start publishing thoughts to the world that could be perceived as foolish, ignorant, insensitive or even racist, coaches will assume you're a knucklehead. In some cases, they could even stop recruiting you. (A cornerback from New Jersey reportedly lost a scholarship from Michigan after a series of sexually explicit and racial tweets.)

This is why many NBA officials tell college coaches to keep their players off of social media. There's just too much risk that in a moment of weakness they'll write something really, really regrettable. So when it comes to social media, I think you'd be wise to follow the advice of Mark Twain: "It is better to remain silent and be thought a fool than to open one's mouth and remove all doubt."

CHAPTER ELEVEN

The Workout: Scrimmaging with the College Team

At a certain point in the recruiting process, depending on the level of the colleges that are recruiting you, you might get a workout with a college coach. Maybe he comes by your high school gym and leads you and a couple of your teammates through a few drills. Or maybe you're on your official visit to a campus, and you're scrimmaging with some of the team's current players.

Whatever the circumstances, these workouts are an important time – a chance for you to prove you're worth a scholarship... or a chance for you to show the coach that you're not quite ready for primetime. (At the JUCO level especially, guys can earn scholarships after 30 minutes of scrimmaging.) So here are a few pointers on how you should behave.

Stay Within Yourself

The biggest thing I always tell kids at these workouts is, "Do what you *can* do. Don't do what you can't do." A lot of kids, when they get in this kind of situation – in the presence of college coaches and players – think they need to be awesome and amazing and wow the coach. So they go out there and try to be spectacular and do things that they've never ever done in any other game, and the end result is they look terrible – wild and ineffective. And then the coach is turned off.

So play your game. Do the things you *can* do, not the things you can't. Coaches don't want to see that you can't post up 15 feet from the basket, Michael Jordan-style, and hit a fadeaway jumper. (If that's your patented move, awesome. But if you've never done that before in a high school game, don't try it now.) Coaches would rather see you catch the ball at the three-point line, take one dribble, one big step right or left, rise up and hit a 15-footer. Simple basketball. Coaches don't expect you to look like Dwyane Wade or Kobe Bryant. They just want to see you play simply. If you consistently make good plays, you'll come off as a great player. If you try to make great plays and fail, you'll come off as a bad player.

Be Smart

In a scrimmage with college players, most high school kids think they need to make shots and score a lot of points to impress the coach. But what ends up happening is, guys take bad shots and play selfish. If a coach has already seen the recruit, he's going to be less critical because he already has something to compare it to. But even still, enough bad plays in a workout might make a coach second-guess that players' ability to play at the college level.

Don't let it come to that. Play smart basketball. I'm not saying you have to defer to the college players in terms of shots. Just make sure the shots you take are the right shots – shots you're comfortable taking. You can still be aggressive. You can still be fearless out there. You should be, actually. Coaches want to see you playing hard and confidently and with toughness. Just don't think if you only score a couple baskets the coach is necessarily going to be disappointed. Coaches would rather see you have an all-around solid performance – good defense, good rebounding, good talk, getting other guys involved, good passes, knocking down shots when they're there – than looking like a ball hog.

Play Good Defense

This is a different sport, but I think the example still holds up. One time Missouri's baseball coach, Tim Jamieson, was scouting players during summer league. He saw a guy named Ian Kinsler – now an All-Star second baseman for the Texas Rangers – taking ground balls and was immediately impressed. Jamieson would later say, "I thought he was as good a middle infielder as I had ever seen. As for his bat, I didn't really care."

Point being: coaches are concerned with how you defend a lot more than you probably think. So when you're at these workouts, focus on good defense just as much as good offense, if not more. Realize that there's this whole other side of the court where you can impress the coach and demonstrate your value for a college team. I'd even go so far as to say that, if all you do is defensively rebound like a beast and consistently find the outlet man, that would be enough to get you in the starting lineup on most college teams in America. How can a coach not want a guy who makes sure the other team only gets one shot (or less)?

Follow Directions

Often during workouts, a guy can't follow the directions of a college coach. A kid will be doing a drill, a coach will give him a little direction, and the kid will go through the drill again... and do it the same way he did it previously. No improvement, no attempt to do it the way the coach just explained. That's a bad sign. As mentioned previously, you want to show that you're coachable. So if a coach tells you to do a drill differently than how you've done it, do it his way. If you don't understand what he's saying, ask for clarification. If you do understand what he's saying but you're not sure you can do it his way, just try as best you can. Go hard and try your best to run it the way he wants.

During individual workouts, half of what I'm looking at is, does he follow directions? Say I have five kids doing a drill. And I demonstrate it, and then I have them do it. I'd rather coach the ones who go and do it as hard as they can, even if they don't do it right, than the one who's kind of passive and doesn't really want to try to do it that way because he knows he's not going to do it right. Even that little bit of information helps me decide if I want a kid or not. Because, what if we're going to run an offense, and this kid doesn't think we can score off this play? Why would I play him if he doesn't believe in what we're going to do? You compare that to the kid who says, "Hey, screw it, I might not do it right, but I'm going to go do it just like coach said." I'll take that kid.

Go Full Speed

Coaches know when you're going hard. And coaches know, if you're going hard and running drills the right way, that you should be tired pretty quickly. If I'm running a big guy through drills, he should be huffing and puffing in two minutes. If he's not, he's not doing them correctly. He's not going as hard as he should be. He's taking six steps where he should be taking three or four. And this is a big turnoff for coaches. Because if a guy seems lazy, coaches are going to pass on him (unless he's just a premier talent) because it's very hard to change that. So the message here is: don't go half-speed through the workout drills. Give it everything you've got. This is your chance to show the coach you know how to work.

Blend In

You have to understand: if a coach brings you in to work out with his team, he *wants* to like you. In fact, he probably already wants you. He just wants to confirm what he already suspects, which is that you've got what it takes to be a good college player. So during the scrimmage, he mostly just wants to see you play with his guys, see how you blend in, see that you look fairly comfortable out there.

Why? Because some kids are talented on the high school level, but they get around college guys, and they've got no confidence and they don't perform well. On the other hand, some guys don't blow you away in high school, but they get in a college scrimmage, where the game is faster and the guys are bigger, and they actually play better. They're not intimidated, they've got confidence, and they know how to play fast. That's what you should strive for. Think of yourself as an equal to these older guys, and play like you belong.

Don't Be Nervous

Take some deep breaths. Warm up the way you would normally warm up. Remind yourself, like that great lesson from *Hoosiers*, that the distance from the floor to the rim is the same height as it is in your high school gym, that the free-throw line is the same distance to the basket, that the court is the same size. And if you are a little nervous, don't worry. It's normal. Just try to turn that nervousness into excitement and energy. Embrace the anxiousness. If you do, you could actually have an advantage over the college guys. Because for them it's just another scrimmage.

And if you're still feeling some butterflies, take a page out of Larry Bird's book. According to legend, Bird, when he stepped to the free-throw line during NBA games, would often think, "I wonder what my grandma is doing right now." It always seemed to calm him down.

CHAPTER TWELVE

Room Service at the Hyatt

So like we said in the last chapter, if you're getting some serious looks from college coaches, at some point you might get invited to campus for a visit. It might be a four-hour trip, or it might be an entire weekend. And you might go on one campus visit or you might go on five. Whatever the circumstances, here's a look at what you can expect...

What the Visit Means

First of all, the fact that a coaching staff is inviting you to campus means they're pretty interested in you. Not that a scholarship offer is guaranteed, but they're definitely considering it at this point. And in some cases, they definitely plan to offer you a scholarship at the end of it. Provided you don't, like, get arrested before Sunday.

You should also know the difference between "official" and "unofficial" campus visits, and recognize which one you're about to embark on. Unofficial visits are all on your dime, and you can take as many of these as you want. The official visit is the all-inclusive paid vacation. That is, the school can pay for travel, food and lodging (for you and your parents). You can take one official visit per school, and you can take a total of five official visits to NCAA D1 and D2 schools, combined.

When It Will Occur

Often your campus visit will occur early on during your senior year, like in October. Schools want to get you in then (especially if you're a highly sought-after recruit) so that they can get you to verbally commit to them while you're on campus, and then sign during the early signing period (which for NCAA basketball is typically in early November). Other times, you'll visit a college after your senior season, like in late March or early April, in the run-up to the regular signing period, which typically goes from mid-April to mid-May. And still other times, they'll bring you in as a junior, and/or in February of your senior year. But the big recruiting visits are going to be in October around the time of Midnight Madness and later in the season before spring signing.

What It Will Entail

It could be as simple as, you drive over with a friend or a parent or a sibling or by yourself and watch one of the team's basketball games. And then the coaches spend a few minutes talking to you after the game. And then you drive home. That's more of the case in an unofficial visit. On an official visit, you'll spend a lot more time on campus. For NCAA and JUCO, an official visit can be up to 48 hours. (NAIA can be up to a month. Kidding!) And the level of luxury you'll be treated to can vary greatly...

At a Major Division I Official Visit...

At major Division I schools, recruits are treated like royalty. When I was a grad assistant at Kansas, we'd put guys up at an expensive hotel in downtown Lawrence, and we'd make mockups of them on the cover of *ESPN The Magazine*, wearing the Jayhawks uniform. (Then the NCAA rules changed, and we had to go digital with the mockups – plastering them on computer screens when the recruit entered a particular room.) Other schools participate in other extravagances – "radio" recordings of a recruit hitting a game-winning shot for the college, his name and image on the gym's scoreboard, a PA announcer screaming his name and measurements in faux pre-game introductions, etc.

The Pampering Can Get Kind of Ridiculous

If you're *really* wanted by a school, they might make sure your favorite food is available at every meal you eat while on campus. There might be signs welcoming you to campus. There might even be signs off the highway on your *way* to campus. It's all a bit much, but it's how the game is played, and virtually every major NCAA Division I program does it, in some capacity or another.

If this kind of love *does* rain down on you, I would say don't take it too seriously and don't make it the basis of your decision. But definitely try to enjoy it, because it's the sort of treatment that you'll experience only once in a lifetime, whether you sign with that particular school or not. (Once you sign, that coach will probably be a lot less warm and fuzzy with you. After all, he still has to coach you. Then it will be all about pushing you and riding you and encouraging you to bring out your best.)

Or You Might Get Very Little Pampering at All

And if you *don't* get this kind of treatment, don't worry about it! It's all a bunch of nonsense anyway, and it has very little to do with how you'll perform on the court once you arrive at college. The one valuable thing it does show you is how much a school really wants you. And it's good to be wanted, because that means a coach believes in you – that you're *his* guy.

Pretty Girls...

There are a few other things you can expect on an official visit to a major D1 school. You might be met by an attractive hostess, an upbeat, sports-minded, biologically gifted college girl who acts as your very own personal guide while you're on campus, taking you from one part of your visit to the next. And she might happen to know about a fun party to check out that night, where some of her equally attractive friends might be in attendance. (Whatever happens, just be smart. And stay away from alcohol and drugs, obviously.)

Big Brothers...

In addition to meeting a hostess, you'll also probably get paired up with some "big brothers" – that is, guys who are currently on the team who will act as mentors while you're visiting. These guys can be a great resource for you. In fact, this is probably where you can find out your best information about a place – what it will really be like going to this school and playing for this coach/team. Definitely feel free to ask them anything you're wondering about. (One good question to ask is, "What's the best part and the worst part about playing here?")

The other thing I'd say is, take note on how you blend with these guys. Obviously, team chemistry will be a huge part of your success at a college, on and off the court. (If you don't like your teammates, you're probably not going to like playing for that team very much.) You should also get a feel for how much these guys embrace you and want you on their team – although they may not fully embrace you until you prove yourself on the court.

Football Games and Handshakes...

If you're visiting in the fall, you'll also probably attend a football game at the school (unless you're visiting, say, Marquette or Georgetown or a place that doesn't really have big-time football). And you'll get a tour of the campus, the weight room, the athletic facilities... maybe a look at a specific academic department and even a professor in that department (or even the *dean* of that department) if you already know what you'd like to study. (While at Kansas, I thought we had a great chance at signing Kyle Singler after I showed him around KU's architecture school and introduced him to the dean of it... but alas, he went to Duke.) If it's a detailed official visit, you might meet with the trainer, the academic monitor and maybe even the athletic director, if he or she is around.

You'll also probably go out with members of the team to a restaurant or two. It's typically a fun weekend, and it'll give you an idea of what you can expect if you end up going to school there. Although, keep in mind, this is a rosier version of the school than you'll likely see if you actually decide to enroll and play there. For one thing, you don't have any homework or classes or grueling practices or conditioning workouts on this visit. And for another thing, everyone won't be on their best behavior around you anymore. But that'll be the same no matter which school you pick.

At Smaller Schools...

At non-major Division I schools, D2 and D3 schools, JUCOs and NAIA colleges, the treatment is much more modest. There's a lot less fanfare, fewer *ESPN The Magazine* cover mockups. And it will usually only last about 24 hours, if that. For example, at my old JUCO, a recruit would arrive on campus around 11:30am on a weekday in the spring. He'd get a tour of the school and the gym, then I'd drive him around town a little and we'd get some lunch. Then I'd show him where his apartment would be, he'd work out with our guys from 3pm to 4:30pm, then we'd go into my office and have our little "talk" (where I might offer him a scholarship or I might not... more on that in a second).

After "The Talk," the recruit would either get back on the road and head for home by about 5:30pm, or he would hang out with a few of the current guys on the team (who would get a few bucks to entertain him), crash on their couch and leave the next day. No fancy hotel and room service at that level. Although, if the kid played his cards right, I might've let him order the baby back ribs at Chili's...

The Talk

So no matter how big the school is or what level the program is at, at some point on a college visit, you and the coach will have "The Talk." Usually this comes at the end of your visit, in the coach's office. (Although really it could happen anytime and anywhere, like at halftime of the football game.)

This is where the coach tells you how he sees you fitting in on the team, answers any questions you may have and, basically, talks about how much he wants you. And he expresses this desire, ideally, in the form of a scholarship offer. ("At this time I want to offer you one of our full basketball scholarships for the upcoming season.") To go back to the dating analogy, it's akin to a guy getting down on his knee and proposing to his girlfriend.

Of course, he might not offer you a full scholarship. He might offer you a partial scholarship. He might offer to pay for your books. (Again, at NCAA Division I, a coach can offer either a full scholarship or no scholarship at all. But at NCAA Division II and JUCOs, he can offer partial scholarships.) Or he may tell you that he can't offer you a scholarship at this time, but he'd really like to have you on his team, and he just needs a bit more time to see how some other things "play out." (Another way you might hear this is, "At this time I don't have a free scholarship I can give you, but one may free up in the future.") The point is, "The Talk" is where you and the coach get down to brass tacks. It's where he spells out – hopefully in very clear English – how much he'd like to have you on his team and what he's willing to offer you in order to make that happen. If you're not understanding exactly what he's offering, be sure to ask him to clarify.

It can also be a pretty exciting moment. Especially if you're finally getting a scholarship offer from a school where you really want to play. (That's the whole idea behind the process... show you how awesome this school and program are, get you excited about attending, and then pop the question, hoping you'll feel overjoyed and say yes.) You might also hear some really nice words of praise from the coach at this point, or he might tell you how he sees your college career playing out at the school. For example, when five-star recruit Dee Brown was thinking about coming to Illinois, Bill Self asked him, "Do you want to be the next poster child for Illinois basketball?" As it turned out, that's exactly what Dee Brown became.

(Note: sometimes The Talk isn't about the offer. The offer has been on the table for a while, in some cases. But The Talk is where the head coach basically earns his money and does his work – and where the best coaches separate themselves from the rest – because at this point it's all about sealing the deal. This is where the salesmanship really comes in – selling that kid on a dream, convincing him that this particular coach and program are going to change his life, and replacing any doubt that kid might have with confidence and excitement. A coach is a salesman, and like any good salesman, he's always closing.)

If They Offer You a Scholarship...

So if the coach does offer you a scholarship during this talk, you've got a decision to make. If the offer comes from an NCAA D1 school, you've got two options, essentially:

1) You can accept. You can say yes and, in the process, "verbally commit" to attending that school and playing for that team. And then when signing day comes, you'll sign a letter-of-intent to play for that college and send it to the college's basketball offices (with or without a press conference at your high school gym). And in the meantime, other coaches from other colleges shouldn't call you. And if they do, you tell them that you're verbally committed to this school, and at that point they should leave you alone.*

*Ideally, anyway. Coaches still might call, if they're really high on you. Or they might go behind your back and try to talk to your mom or your grandma or your best friend or your girlfriend or your uncle. This is not considered great behavior by coaches, but it definitely happens. Obviously, it happens more often with the really premier blue-chip recruits. So if coaches are doing this for you, you should take it as a good sign that they think a lot of you.**

**But you should still try to keep getting better as a player. There are plenty of premier, blue-chip high school recruits who didn't distinguish themselves at the college level and never played a minute of pro basketball.

2) Or you can say, basically, "Cool, Coach. Let me think about it." Although you might want to express this with a little more enthusiasm and finesse. Like: "Hey, that's great, Coach, I really appreciate this. There are still a few other schools I want to check out, but I definitely appreciate this offer, and I will let you know as soon as possible." (And if this is your answer, be ready for more salesmanship and courting from the coach.)

For a D1 scholarship offer, those are pretty much your only two options for responses. Obviously, you could also just say, "No thanks." But if you were interested enough to go on the campus visit, you probably wouldn't say this. (Unless of course you just had a terrible time on your visit, for some reason. Like, the coaches were jerks, the current players ignored you, and you got food poisoning from the room service. Then it might be understandable if you just said, "Thanks but no thanks, Coach.")

For JUCO...

Now, if you get a scholarship offer from a JUCO, and the offer happens to come during a signing period, you actually have a third option. You can go ahead and sign your letter-of-intent right there on the spot. (And, as Larry the Cable Guy might say, "get 'er done.") (Note: Did I just make a Larry the Cable Guy reference? I apologize.) Again, this is something you're not allowed to do at an NCAA Division I school. (Although I've seen it happen. And then I've seen that coaching staff get fired.)

If You Change Your Mind...

One other thing: if you verbally commit to a school but then, a few days or a few weeks or a few months later, you start to have (major) second thoughts about your decision, one thing you can do is "reopen your recruiting" or "de-commit." In that case, just tell the coach that you'd like to reopen your recruiting because you'd like to take a look at other schools.

This kind of thing happens. It's not what the school that offered you a scholarship wants to hear and it doesn't happen very often (it happens more in football, I think), but it happens. Whatever the reason for your change of heart, it's much better to be upfront with the school like this than to not tell them anything and visit another school anyway. Because they will find out. And this is basically like "cheating" on a school, which is a no-no. "Reopening your recruiting" is more like asking to see other people, which is considered the more honest, mature way to handle your decision/indecision.

When you tell a school you'd like to reopen your recruiting, they're not going to be happy. And they'll try to talk you out of it. But eventually, if you stick to your guns, they'll probably say, "OK, go check out that other place, but we still want you and we still think this is the best place for you." And then you'll go take that other visit (or two or three) and make up your mind. You might decide that you like the original school the best after all. And you might feel better about your decision now that you've checked out your other options (and realized that the grass wasn't greener).

On the other hand, you might reopen your recruiting, go visit this other school and come away thinking, "Yeah, this other school is way better for me. I really want to go here." You might even think, "What was I doing giving a verbal commitment to that first school? The town sucked and the coach was scary."

Having said all that, I'd say this: to avoid this kind of situation, take all your scheduled official visits before committing to one school. Or barring that, don't commit to a school if you've still got other official visits to take unless you've got a *great* feeling about the place and you know in your heart it's the right place for you (and you get the offer you want).

Once you officially commit to a school, be confident with your decision and stand by it. (Unless there's, say, a coaching change at that school or some kind of scandal.) Hopefully if you've done your homework – and read this book – you will make the right decision and stick with it.

And if you're the type of guy who's getting a lot of scholarship offers but doesn't particularly enjoy the recruiting process, I would suggest you visit your favorite school first, so that if you find what you want, you can stop your search sooner rather than later.

CHAPTER THIRTEEN

Essential Questions: The Six Things You Have to Ask a Coach

Before you can make an educated decision on your future, you have to, you know, educate yourself. Meaning: you have to put on your journalist hat and gather as much information as you can on the programs that you're considering. There are a ton of questions you can (and should) ask, but in my opinion, there are half a dozen queries that you absolutely have to get answers to before you can make an informed decision. They are...

What will I have to pay for?

If you're offered a scholarship from a college, you have to make sure you're clear on how much the scholarship covers. And phrasing the question like this – "What will I have to pay for?" – eliminates any room for coaches to deceive/confuse you. Because a coach might tell you that he's giving you a full scholarship, but it might turn out that that coach is at a D2 JUCO, and to him, a "full scholarship" only includes tuition and books, not room and board. (Yes, I've heard of this happening.) So this is a really important question to ask, because you don't want any major financial surprises after you've already signed a letter-of-intent.

If I qualify for a Pell Grant, do I get to keep it?

This is a huge one, and one that most people don't know about. If you fill out your FAFSA form (which you can do at fafsa.ed.gov with the help of a parent) and it comes back that you are a full Pell Grant qualifier, that means you are entitled to the maximum Pell Grant each year, which is now $5,500. Basically, that's free money that you don't have to pay back, every year. Let me repeat: that's free money that you don't have to pay back, every year! It goes in your pocket and you can use it for miscellaneous expenses – school supplies, extra meals on the weekend, transportation, entertainment, maybe a gift here and there. (Or, you could just put it in the bank and by the time you graduate, you could have over $20,000. Just saying.)

But here's the catch. Some schools may give you a full scholarship but keep your Pell Grant. So you might get everything paid for, but that $5,500 will go to the school to help pay for your living expenses each year. Now, most major NCAA D1 schools let you keep your Pell Grant, as do some JUCO D1s. (And typically, if they do let you keep it, they'll advertise that fact because they want you to know how good of a deal you're getting.) But other schools (like some NCAA D2s and NAIA schools) take your Pell Grant. It might seem a little cold-blooded and unfair, but it's totally within their rights. So again, you just want to ask about this and make sure you're clear on this issue before you sign. Because it's essentially a $22,000 question.

How do you see me fitting into your team, as far as playing time, position and style of play?

This is a crucial question, and it addresses a few concerns: one, how much playing time are you going to get, both right away and throughout your career; two, where and how will you be used; and three, what is the team's style of play, which you need to know to make sure it's a style you are comfortable with and suited for.

Now, anytime the question of minutes or "starting" comes up, most coaches are going to give the same stock answer, more or less. That answer goes like this: "I don't guarantee starting spots for anybody. Just because somebody started the previous year doesn't mean they'll start this year. I play the guys who make us the best team on the court, plain and simple. You have to earn a starting spot every week, and every day, in practice." That answer could also include: "I want any guy I bring in to come in and work hard and demand minutes. I wouldn't be offering you a scholarship unless I planned to play you."

All of that is true. But the fact is, a team can have up to 13 guys on scholarship. And only five guys can play at a time. So somebody's going to be on the bench. So you'll want to pay attention to what else the coach says when he answers that question, because that could be revealing. He might say, "If you come in and play the way I think you're capable of playing, I see you playing lots of minutes right away for this team." Or he might say, "We've got a lot of guys right now. But after next year, some of those guys will be gone. That's when I really see you making an impact for us."

In the first case, the coach is essentially saying he sees you playing 30 minutes a game, maybe starting (assuming you fight for playing time the way he thinks you can). In the second case, the coach is saying he sees you playing 5-10 minutes a game as a freshman, but with the chance to play a lot more after that.

But it will also be valuable to hear how he thinks you'll be used, as far as position and role. Does he see you as a scorer, a distributor, a point guard, a two guard, a swing man, a big, a guy who will "bang," do the "dirty work," rebound, score in the paint, get a lot of dunks, be "the man," be "the poster boy," be a "glue guy," a "pest," a "contributor," what? And how well does his impression of you match up with your own impression of yourself – and who you want to become? Does he "get you" as a player? (Again, just like in dating, it's really important that you feel like this person "gets" you.) Also: would he motivate you? Would he bring the best out in you?

Of course, the other thing you can (and should) do is your own research. Who do they have coming back at your position? How good are these guys, and what years are they? Are they All-Conference players who will be sophomores next year (which might not bode well for you, as far as minutes), or are they so-so players who will be seniors next year anyway?

Another thing to research: how many guys does this coach usually play? Does he play seven a game or does he play eleven a game? Who else are they recruiting? What *is* the team's style of play? Would you like to play this style? Does it suit your skills? You might love the coach, but if the style of play doesn't fit your game at all, you probably shouldn't go there.

What academic resources are available to me?

Obviously, you want to stay academically eligible. You'd also like to learn skills that will help you in life and in a future career. So you want to find out what resources are in place to help you with schoolwork. Do they have tutors? How are their tutors set up? Will you have one tutor for all (or most) of your classes, or will you have a different tutor for each class? Do these tutors work only with student-athletes, or are these campus-wide tutors who are in high demand and may be difficult to track down? It's good to know that stuff.

Of course, you may be great at academics and this may not apply to you. But even if you were a strong high school student, college can be a big adjustment and a big challenge. Especially with the massive hours you'll be devoting to basketball, year-round.

How will I be developed, and how many guys have you sent to the next level?

The first part of this question speaks to how you'll grow as a player and an athlete while you're at college. You want to hear what kind of weight program they've got, what their strength coach has done (if they have a strength coach), what their strength-training philosophy is (is it traditional Olympic-style weight lifting or more new-wave, "functional" training) and how this training has helped past players and some of the older guys on the team.

For example, a coach might say, "Our 6-10 center went from 215 to 235 pounds over the summer, adding 20 pounds of pure muscle, because our strength trainer had him on this program that she picked up while assisting the U.S. basketball team." This would be a great thing to hear, especially if you're an undersized big man. (And you'll want to verify this information somehow – ideally with the 6'10" center himself.)

You also want to hear about what kind of nutrition program they've got, and what they would like to do with you, on and off the court, to enhance your skills and make you a better player over the next two to four years.

Note: this is also something you could ask current players about – "Do you think the coaching staff has helped you become a better player? A better athlete? How so?" And you'll also want to do your own research. Look at guys on his team over the past four years and ask yourself: do players seem to get better under this coach, or worse?

The second part of this question – how many guys have you sent to the next level? – speaks to the program's track record of getting guys to the pros. Or, if it's a JUCO, its track record of sending guys to four-year schools to play. Obviously, the more success stories they've got, the better you'll probably feel about your chances for doing the same. Yes, scouts will find you if you're good enough, but it helps if your coach has connections to people in the pros or people at NCAA D1 and D2 schools.

So if you're considering a JUCO, ask yourself: is this JUCO a factory for NCAA D1 and D2 schools, or has it not sent a guy to a D1 or D2 school in the past five years? If it hasn't (and you really *want* to play D1 or D2 basketball), that would probably make you think twice about going to that JUCO. (The other thing that's especially true with JUCOs is that the JUCOs with the best records and the ones that consistently go to the national tournament are the ones that send the most guys to four-year schools. So if you're at a JUCO that doesn't have a very good record, even if you're pretty good, you really could go undiscovered.)

How long do you plan to be here, Coach?

Obviously, you're asking this because you want to make sure this coach who you like will be sticking around to coach you.

Now, you may not get a completely honest answer. I don't think any coach is going to say, "My goal is to be gone next year." But the way the coach answers this question could tell you a little bit about how committed he is to his current job. He may say, "I plan to be here for a long, long time." Or he may say, "There's only one other job I'd rather have. And Coach K isn't going anywhere." Or he may say, "I'll be here as long as they'll have me. This is my dream job." (Which might be true until an even bigger dream job opens up.)

The fact is, you'll never know for sure if the coach at the school you're picking will be there for your entire college career. You know why? Because the *coach* doesn't even know. The coaching profession is so much of a roller coaster. One day there are no jobs open, and then the next day a coach gets fired and another coach takes his place, and then another coach takes *that* guy's place, and suddenly there's an opening at a place a coach never thought there'd be an opening at. And if it's the right fit for the coach (and a better job), then you can't fault him for entertaining that.

But there are, often, some warning signs. Which you can spot if you do your homework. Ask yourself this: does this coach have a history of leaving after a few years? Is there another job that's available that he might want? Is his name on ESPN every other day about a possible vacancy (either in college or the pros)? On the flip side: has he had three mediocre seasons in a row? Are there rumblings from the fan base that this is his last season to get it right? Any of those things might give you pause about a particular coach. (You can also check the internet. Websites like hoopdirt.com report fairly accurate information/rumors about coaching situations.)

Or, at the end of the day, you might decide it's worth the risk. You might think, "Hey, it's a good scholarship offer to a good school. Even if the coach does end up leaving, I'm sure they'll bring in another guy who knows what he's doing." Depending on your other options and how much you like this coach and school, that might be a good way to look at it.

CHAPTER FOURTEEN

Other Great Questions to Ask

Last chapter we talked about six essential questions to ask a college coach. Here are some other good – though not essential – things to ask him. Remember, the more information you have, the better decision you can make about your future.

Do you offer four-year scholarships, and can I have one?

Technically, an athletic scholarship – even a full athletic scholarship at an NCAA D1 school – is only good for one year, not four years. Most major D1 schools honor it for four years, unless you do something stupid and/or illegal and get yourself kicked off the team. But they don't have to. And sometimes, if a player is not "working out" at a school (that is, not playing very much or very effectively), a coach will encourage him to pursue transfer options. And sometimes (not very often, but sometimes), a coach will flat-out inform a player that his scholarship will not be renewed for next year. Likewise, a scholarship at a JUCO is technically only valid for one year, not two years. After each year, the coach has the right to renew a player's scholarship for another year – or not.

But just recently (like, February of 2012), the NCAA passed a rule allowing schools the option to offer four-year scholarships in addition to single-year, renewable scholarships. Most football programs in the Big 10 actually offered four-year scholarships to their 2012 recruiting classes. Now, the jury is still out on how many schools will offer these four-year scholarships for basketball (and how long this rule change will last). But it's definitely worth asking about (why settle for one when you can get four?), and you may want to make this part of your decision-making process.

For example, if Washington State is offering you a four-year scholarship and Washington is only willing to offer you a one-year scholarship, you might want to go with the Cougars over the Huskies, for security reasons and peace of mind about your future. Especially if all else is relatively equal (you like both coaches, both programs, etc.), and you're concerned you might not get your scholarship renewed at UW. On the other hand, if you've got a lot of confidence that you're the next Nate Robinson, you might just decide to bet on yourself and go with the Huskies anyway, knowing that you'll prove yourself valuable enough to receive a new scholarship each season.

(Also: it's not like that four-year scholarship is bulletproof. If you quit the team or flunk out of school or get arrested, you can lose that four-year deal just as quickly as a one-year deal.)

Do you provide a fifth year of scholarship?

Say you play four years of basketball at a school. And for some reason, no pro teams are blowing up your cell phone for a tryout. If you haven't graduated yet but you want to (and you should want to… assuming you're a fan of jobs and money), then a scholarship for a fifth year of school would be very useful. So you can ask the school: will I get a scholarship for my fifth year, after my eligibility is up?

Sometimes schools can't do it or won't do it. They just don't have the budget for it. But other schools – again, usually major D1 schools – will pick up a fifth year of scholarship for a player. For example, when I was at Illinois, I got a year and a half worth of scholarship as a player. But then Illinois gave me a scholarship for my entire fifth year of school, even though I didn't play on the team anymore. By NCAA rules, you're allowed to do this, and it doesn't count against a team's 13 scholarships. (And again, if you qualify for a full Pell Grant, that's *another* $5,500 you could receive. Which means you could really walk away with nearly $30,000 after five years of college, if you throw it all in the bank and earn some decent interest.)

Now, I should probably also say this: to ask about a fifth year of scholarship – as a senior in high school – might be viewed as kind of presumptuous or "putting the cart before the horse" on your part. But go ahead and ask, if you want. A coach will probably be impressed that you're looking that far into the future.

Will you help me get a job after I graduate?

Again, it might seem a little early to already be asking your potential coach if he can hook you up with a job. But hey, if I had a son who was getting recruited by schools, this is something I'd like to know. I mean, it's definitely something that regular students think about when they're considering attending a college – what resources and connections does this school have to help put me on the right path, career-wise, after I graduate?

So especially if you're getting seriously recruited by three or four schools (or more), feel free to ask about this. This will give the coach a chance to talk about any sort of network of alumni who are available and eager to help out former players. And it'll also give the coach a chance to cite specific examples of former players who are now working for people or companies that are so-called "friends of the program."

For example, if I had a son who was interested in sports management, I'd want to ask that coach, do you know any sports management companies or sports agencies that might be able to give him an internship or an entry-level job after graduation? This is the type of thing that most recruits don't ask about, but really, they probably should. For one thing, this recruiting period, as funny as it sounds, might be one of your best chances to have this much one-on-one time with a coach. And secondly, you'll be amazed how fast four years will go by and you'll be out there looking for a job. Obviously you could ask your coach about an internship or a job when you're closer to graduation, but it doesn't hurt to lay the groundwork early.

And plus, it's a lot more helpful to hear, "No, sorry, I have no connections at sports management companies" *now* than it is to hear it after you've poured four years of blood, sweat and tears into this guy's program.

Which assistant coach will work with me the most?

If the program has a full stable of assistant coaches, you'll want to find out which ones work with the guards, which ones work with the bigs and which one is going to be working with you the most. In other words, find out who's going to be "your" assistant. And then you'll want to ask yourself, do I like this guy? Could I work hard for this guy? Could he motivate me? Could he teach me things? Because, especially at the bigger schools, the assistant coaches are a major part of the program and the team. Don't undervalue them when deciding on a school.

You should probably find out a little bit about the assistants – their backgrounds and their coaching style or philosophy. (For one thing, definitely ask current players how they like working with them.) If you decide you like the head coach but can't stand the assistant coach who's going to be working with you on a daily basis, that school might not be the best option for you. Because you'll actually be spending lots of time with the assistant coach – in some cases, as much or more than with the head coach. (This is even more true for football players. If you happen to be a two-sport star reading this.)

Then again, you have to realize, no situation is going to be perfect. Depending on what other scholarship offers you have, you might want to just learn to deal with this guy, even if he's not your favorite person.

CHAPTER FIFTEEN

Even More Great Questions to Ask

Here are some other questions that you'll want to find answers to. Now, I'm not saying you should ask the head coach about all these things. Some of them you can find out on your own by doing a little homework. Others you can find out by asking assistant coaches or current players. (Or maybe even attractive girls you meet at parties while on campus visits...) You also might notice that some of these questions are repeats from earlier in the book. I just want to make sure you have them all in one place.

- How many students go to the school?
- How far away is it from my hometown?
- Does it have the academic program I'm interested in pursuing?
- Where will I live? In a dorm or an off-campus apartment? Or an eight-bedroom duplex?
- Is a cafeteria and meal plan included at this place?
- How is the town? What do the current players do for fun? (Ask them.) Could I live there?
- How many fans come to the games? How's the atmosphere in the arena?
- What's the situation at the gym – can I go to it any time of day, punch in a code and get access to work out, or is it only available at certain times? (Quick story: one of my former junior-college players ultimately chose one four-year school over two others because he liked that the apartments

were really close to the gym, and the gym was available 24 hours a day to shoot around in. All he had to do was type in a code.)

- As far as the team, how many starters are returning? How many returners play the same position as me? How many guys are they signing this year?
- Would I be able to come in and play right away? (I know we mentioned this two chapters ago, but it bears repeating. And this question is especially important for guys going to JUCOs, because you have only two years, max.)
- What was their record last year? What is the coach's overall record? Has the program been winning the last few years, or losing? (Are they on the rise or on the decline?)
- Do the current players like the head coach? The assistants? (Ask them.)
- What's their style of play?
- How's the weight room? Strength coach? Strength program?
- How is the school spirit in regards to basketball?
- Would I like playing with the current players that I met?
- Can I develop into a great player here, from what I've seen?
- How's the conference? What's the level of the other schools in the conference? What's the atmosphere like at their gyms?
- Who are their main rivals? What are the atmospheres like at these gyms?
- How often is this team on regional television? National television?
- Would I have a chance to play in postseason tournaments?
- Would I have a chance to develop into a pro player here?
- How do I look in their uniform? (Kidding... kind of.)

CHAPTER SIXTEEN

The Backup Plan: Walking On

So let's say you're cruising through your high school basketball career. You're a good player. You start for your team. You put up solid numbers. You're a key contributor and a guy that other teams don't want to face. But you haven't gotten a sniff from college coaches. Not one letter, not one call, not one Twitter direct-message.

So you send emails. You send links to your edit tape on YouTube. You call coaches and assistant coaches. You play in showcase games after your senior year. You try everything we've talked about in this book. You tell anyone who will listen that you've got a passion for the game and you're determined to play in college. And still: nothing. Nada. Bupkis.

Well, good news: the door is not completely closed. There's another option available to you: you can be a walk-on. That is, a guy who's on a college team but doesn't have an athletic scholarship. Usually, this means the guy doesn't play much (if at all). He's a practice player, usually. He suits up but he doesn't get in the game, unless the game is lopsided and he's brought in for mop-up duty. At least, that's the stereotype of a walk-on.

But as mentioned earlier in this book, there are exceptions. Sometimes walk-ons get in the game. Sometimes they get meaningful minutes. Sometimes they start. Sometimes they close. Sometimes they earn scholarships.

Sometimes they score 18 points a game. Sometimes they go on to play in the pros (while their more highly recruited college teammates don't). It happens. Not very often, but it happens.

So if this sounds like something you might be interested in, then this chapter is for you. And I should mention: I definitely have a lot to say on this subject – because I used to be a walk-on myself…

Step One: Make Your Intentions Known

It's not like you can just snap your fingers and become a walk-on at the college of your choice. In most cases, you actually have to fight to become one. Although in a few cases, you might get invited to try out as a "preferred walk-on."

Either way, the first step is to think about where you'd like to be a walk-on. (In my case, that was the University of Illinois, my hometown team.) Once you've decided on that, the next step is to apply and get accepted there. Once you've done *that*, the next step is to reach out to the head coach (either by phone, email or letter… or all three) and make your intentions known. In other words, tell him that you'd like to walk on to his basketball team next season. This will probably be sometime late in your senior year.

Assuming you get ahold of the coach, he will probably tell you something like, "OK, you're welcome to try out to be a walk-on. We'll be holding tryouts in the fall. Call back closer to September and we'll give you the date." (There's a small chance he'll say, "Sorry, we're not having walk-on tryouts this year," although that's pretty unlikely. Typically schools still hold walk-on tryouts, even if they don't plan to take anyone. Reason being, coaches never know when they might find that diamond in the rough. One season at Parkland, I had a 6'7" Belgian student walk into my gym, out of the blue, asking to try out. By the end of the season he was starting for me.)

If you don't hear back at all from the coach, keep calling, writing and emailing. You might even try to pop by his office or an assistant coach's office or the basketball team's office and see what you can find. (Sometimes in life, the only way to get something done is to go there in person.)

In My Case...

Quick story about me. I was a three-year starter and scored about 15 points per game my senior year at Champaign Central High, and I didn't get any interest from colleges. I think I might have gotten one letter from a D3 school, although that might have been for baseball. I certainly didn't get any scholarship offers – not even from the local junior college where I ended up coaching.

So late in my senior year, I reached out to the Illinois coach at the time, Lon Kruger. Coach Kruger was generous enough to invite my parents and me to his office for about a 15-minute chat. I told him that I was planning to attend Illinois in the fall and that I wanted to walk on to the team. He didn't make any promises, but he said I was welcome to try out. That was really all I wanted – a chance.

Step Two: Prepare for the Tryout

OK, back to you. That spring and summer, you should really be trying to get in good shape. If you're a big guy and you need to slim down, slim down. (Work out every day and cut out the junk food and soft drinks.) If you're a small guy and you need to bulk up, bulk up. (Hit the weights, drink protein shakes, etc.)

But the other thing you should definitely do is play as much basketball as you can before the tryout. And not just basketball – high-quality, competitive basketball. Ideally, you'll find out where the current players on the team are playing during the summer and try to work out with them. This will serve a couple of purposes. One, you'll become a better player simply by playing with them. And two, assuming you hold your own against them, they'll start to trust you. And come tryouts, they'll be pulling for you. They might even put in a good word with the coaches.

Again, to bring it back to me for a second, this is what I did the summer before my freshman year at Illinois, and it helped a lot. I know I earned some respect from the current players, and I got a better feel for how guys played in college.

(Note: if you can't work out with the current players on the team because you don't live in that town yet, you should try to find other competitive games to play in. Maybe there's another college near you, and you can play with those guys. Maybe there's an open gym at your high school. Maybe there's an ex-teammate you can work out with. Maybe, like Jimmer Fredette, there's a prison game that's open to non-prisoners. Bottom line: find a high-level game and play in it on a regular basis.)

Step Three: Do the Team Conditioning Drills in the Fall

Before the tryout for walk-ons, the team will probably start doing some organized conditioning work on their own. Now, you probably won't be able to do this stuff with them because you're not a member of the team. So you should do the next best thing: find out what they're doing and replicate it on your own. How do you find out what they're doing? Ask one of the current players that you've befriended during your pickup games over the summer. Or do a little detective work...

Back to Me...

When I was preparing for the walk-on tryout at Illinois, I would actually show up to the team's conditioning runs in the early morning on the U of I's campus, sit on a staircase near them and write down everything they did. Then I'd go do it on my own. I think the guys on the team and the coaches might've thought I was a little nutty, but hey, sometimes you gotta be a little nutty in life to get ahead. The worst thing the coaches could have done was ask me to leave. And they never did.

Step Four: Have a Great Tryout

So then the big day will arrive. There might be nine other guys you're competing against for one spot. There might be 30 other guys you're competing against for two spots. There might be 50 guys out there and no guarantee that even one guy will make the team.

Whatever the case may be, just make sure you leave it all out there. Work hard, show enthusiasm, demonstrate desire, be aggressive. You might even want to play with a little fire, a little chip on your shoulder. The coaches are looking for guys to provide energy in practice, so if you can't provide it in the walk-on tryout, that's going to be a big turnoff. So be relentless for however long that tryout is – 90 minutes or whatever. Dive for loose balls, show how much you want it. Don't back down from anybody. And make a few shots while you're at it.

(Also: don't worry about being the worst guy out there. Trust me, there'll be someone worse than you out there. Even at Illinois and Kansas, every year there were guys trying out to be walk-ons who had no business being on a college basketball court. It's sort of equivalent to those people who try out for *American Idol* even though they can't sing a lick.)

Back to Me...

At my walk-on tryout, a couple things stand out. One, some of the current players were on hand, and they were kind of rooting for me because I'd been playing with a lot of them all summer. And two, I was told later that one of the things Coach Kruger said he liked about me was that I played with a chip on my shoulder. But I think you have to play with a chip on your shoulder in a situation like that. You're literally competing against these guys for a spot on the team – in this case, a major D1 basketball team! You don't want to get in any fights, but you want to play really hard. Don't save anything for tomorrow because there might not be one.

And hey, if you don't make it, at least you'll never wonder if you could have if you'd tried. And there's always next year...

CHAPTER SEVENTEEN

The Highs and Lows of Being a Walk-On

Now, maybe you're trying to decide between accepting a scholarship to a small school or walking on at a big school. Or maybe you're trying to decide between walking on at a big school or calling it a career, playing college intramurals and cheering for the team from the stands. Whatever the case may be, here are some things you should know about being a walk-on – both good and bad. Again, I can definitely speak from personal experience on this topic.

Let's start with the advantages…

Lots of Gear

If you're a walk-on at a major D1 school, you get all the gear. You get the warm-ups, the sweats, the shoes, the T-shirts, the shorts, the travel warm-ups, the jackets. If you play in any of the bigger preseason tournaments, sometimes there are gifts like iPod shuffles and Best Buy gift cards and all that.

Travel

If you're at a bigger school, you get to take private planes and chartered buses around the region and the country. When I was at Illinois, I got to go to Australia for a summer tour and Maui for a preseason tournament. Two places I probably would have never gone to otherwise.

"Fame"

You're on TV (even if you're just sitting on a bench or springing off of it at timeouts to high-five teammates). You're representing your school, which gives you recognition off the court and a certain amount of respect. It also gives you a certain amount of fame – at least on a local level – whether you want it or not.

You might get the occasional newspaper or TV interview, too. On media day, you might be asked what it's like to guard so and so in practice, what your outlook on the season is, etc. If you're an attention hound or a face jock, you'll probably eat this stuff up.

Career

Being a walk-on could actually lead you to a better life, if your school has alumni that like to take care of people who played college sports. You might meet a friend of the program at a post-season banquet who can hook you up with a job. Or you might distinguish yourself on a job interview because it says on your resume that you played college basketball – and maybe the person doing the hiring happens to be a big fan of the school where you played.

Or it can be a great foundation for a career in coaching. Think about it: as a walk-on, you have four years to soak up all the basketball knowledge you can. You get to see how a college coach handles practices, games, pre-game speeches and everything else. It's sort of like the best unpaid internship you could get. That's basically what happened in my case. After college, I followed Coach Self (who had replaced Coach Kruger) to Kansas, where I was a grad assistant for the basketball team and earned my master's in architecture. That led to a job as an assistant coach at a D1 JUCO in Arkansas, which led to a head coach job at Parkland, which led to my Director of Basketball Operations position at Southern Illinois.

Special Treatment

Even if you're a walk-on, you probably have an academic advisor that takes care of all of your classes, so you don't have to go meet with a regular advisor and wait in lines and all that stuff. (You might also have an easier time getting into popular classes.) You have the chance to earn an athletic scholarship. And even if you don't, you can get "per diem" money when the team goes on trips. So you're actually making a little bit of money by being on the team because you do get money for traveling.

Excitement

You're part of the program. It's exciting. You're on the court in front of thousands of screaming fans. You're right there when your coach is drawing up the last-second play. You're storming the court when your team wins at the buzzer. You're part of March Madness. You go to the Sweet Sixteen. The Elite Eight. Maybe even the Final Four. You're rubbing elbows with Bill Raftery and Jay Bilas and Dick Vitale. (It's awesome, baby!)

Chance for Playing Time

And there's always the chance you could actually play in games. My sophomore year, a key guy had to sit out the entire season because he wasn't cleared by the NCAA, and I actually started four games. (Had 5 points and 5 assists against Michigan State! Take that, Mateen Cleaves!) Other walk-ons have had significantly more success. Jeff Hornacek went from a walk-on at Iowa State to the star of the team and an NBA All-Star (and one of the best forehead-wiping free-throw shooters in NBA history). Scottie Pippen went from walking on at a tiny NAIA school in Arkansas to winning six NBA championships and being named one of the 50 best players of all time. Not bad. Not bad at all.

Now to the disadvantages...

Immobility

You might not get to go on all those trips. You might not get to travel (or get the much-coveted travel per diem). You might not even get to dress for all the home games. My freshman year, I didn't get to travel at all, and I only got to dress every third home game. (I know: poor me.)

Second-Class Citizen

And even if you do get to travel and dress for all the games, you might not feel like you're treated as well as the scholarship guys. Because you weren't recruited to be on the team. And because you don't, like, play very much. Now I'm not saying that's true for every walk-on because, as mentioned earlier, some walk-ons end up playing meaningful minutes.

Practice Dummy

In practice, you are expected to do a lot of the dirty work. You might be used as the dummy defense, where you just have to guard guys for a whole drill just to let them work on their offense. Or you might have to be the guy who's holding the rebounding pad while the scholarship players are working on finishing with contact. So you don't necessarily get the fun side of the drills – or the part that helps you improve your game.

Fewer Reps

And sometimes you don't get to practice at all. You might be standing on the sideline for a lot of the practice, until the coaches are ready to use you, and then you suddenly get called in and you have to be ready to go. And then five minutes later you're out again.

Punchlines

Often the walk-ons bear the brunt of the jokes and the criticism on the team. Usually one assistant coach in particular tends to make fun of the walk-ons, staying on their case and making them the scapegoat for anything that goes wrong during practice. So as a walk-on, you just have to know that an assistant coach is probably going to ride you. One, to make an example of you. And two, to entertain everybody else.

Lots of Time and Energy

Being a walk-on is a huge time commitment. You're practicing every day, you're traveling, you're working out in the weight room. So you just have to know that going in and embrace it. You can't go halfway with it.

Little Game Time

The average walk-on at a D1 school might play a total of 20 minutes all season. And even then, it's still probably what you'd call "mop-up duty." If you're looking for real, actual playing time, you might want to think about walking on at a smaller school – where you could maybe be a preferred walk-on. (Or as I mentioned at the top, you might want to think about being a star on your dorm team or your fraternity team or your church-league team.)

But if you just want to be a part of a big-time program and you don't care so much about playing time, I'm here to tell you that there's nothing better than being a walk-on at a major D1 school. And if you do get meaningful minutes, you've got to forget that you're a walk-on, let everything go and just play.

CHAPTER EIGHTEEN

If He Says This, It Means This: Dissecting "Coach Speak"

One of the most important parts of the recruiting process is understanding what college coaches are telling you. Which can sometimes be incredibly challenging! In general, coaches, much like politicians, don't want to back themselves into a corner or commit too strongly to a particular stance, for fear of limiting their future options. (See? I even did it in that previous sentence, by saying "in general.") So often their statements take some decoding. Here are some things a college coach might say to you during the recruiting process, and here's what each statement generally means. Consider this your Coach-to-English dictionary...

If You Hear This...

"We like you. We're not ready to offer you a scholarship right now. We're looking at a couple of other guys. I should have an answer for you in a couple of weeks."

It Means...

You're a Tier 2 guy, at best, in their eyes. See, coaches have tiers – Tier 1, Tier 2 and Tier 3. Tier 1 guys are guys who coaches would love to get, but they know they might not get them because everybody is recruiting them and these players may be out of their league. Tier 2 guys are guys who coaches would like to have and will probably offer a scholarship to – if all of their Tier 1 guys fall through. Tier 3 guys are guys whom they don't really want, but they may end up needing late in the recruiting process when they've missed on Tier 1 guys and even their Tier 2 guys have gone elsewhere.

So if you hear the above, it means you'll definitely want to keep your recruiting options open. This coach might have an offer for you, but there are definitely guys ahead of you. So the smart thing for you to do would be, if other schools are talking to you, keep talking to them. Don't think, "Oh, I'm going to get an offer from this school in a couple of weeks. The coach basically said so." Because if you listened carefully, he really didn't. He might call back in two weeks and say he can't offer you anything after all. Or he might call back in three weeks and say he can't offer you anything after all. Or he might not call back at all!

If anything, you should try to ramp up your recruiting with those other schools that are interested in you. See if you can go visit them if you haven't already. That way you have some leverage with the above coach. He knows you've visited this other school and you can actually make him a little jealous. Think about it: who's a coach going to want more, the guy who's not getting recruited by anyone else, or the guy who's getting recruited by three other schools – one of which happens to be his biggest rival? Of course it's the latter.

So, just like a girl who starts talking to other guys to increase the attention of the guy she really wants, you should start talking to other schools. This is how you can use the system to your advantage, play on the coach's fears and make him worried he's going to lose you to a team he dislikes – and a team he's going to have to play two or three times a year – if he doesn't act fast.

A final important point here is: even though you might not be a school's top choice, that doesn't mean it's necessarily the wrong school for you. Lots and lots of players have had a ton of success at schools where they weren't initially considered a top prospect. It's sort of like an actor landing a great movie role after a bigger-name actor turned down the part. Just because you weren't the producer's first pick doesn't mean you both can't make a great movie together.

If You Hear This...

"How is your recruiting going? Who else is talking to you?"

It Means...

"Who else thinks you're good, and how many people am I going to have to beat out to get you?" Again, the more schools you mention that you're talking to – and the more "good" schools you mention – the more that coach is going to be interested in you. Coaches are busy, so they often rely on the opinions of other coaches to save time. The result is they end up being copycats. If a kid is wanted by two schools, he'll suddenly be wanted by six schools. If a kid isn't wanted by any schools, then a coach will assume he must not be very good. Even if he watches him and sees him play well. (*I must have seen him on his best day. He must not normally play like that.*)

So if there are other schools that you've been talking to, you definitely want to mention them to that coach when he asks you how your recruiting is going. You don't want to ever lie and say you're talking to a school that you're actually not (because a coach will find out, and that will reflect poorly on your character), but you definitely want to make it known who else has shown interest in you, and how interested they are.

Because here's the thing: if a coach hears that a kid is being recruited by three or four schools that are as good or better than his school, he is most likely going to start recruiting that kid (or at least take a serious look at him). It's the same as an eligible young woman saying, "On Wednesday Chad called, and on Thursday Bill called, and on Friday I went out with Steve, and Sam calls me all the time, practically every night." That's going to make the typical guy furious – but also much more interested in winning her.

Final comment on this: it's helpful to know which schools this coach might view as competitors. If you say a weaker school, that coach might think, "Go ahead and go there; we typically beat that school anyway."

If You Hear This...

"You've got to let me know within the next three days, or the scholarship's off the table."

It Means...

They want you, but they also want this next-in-line kid who they might lose. So they're going to pressure you into making a decision so that if you say no, they still have time to get the next-in-line guy.

But it also might be a bluff. They might just want you to hurry up and say yes. Especially if it's late in the recruiting period, when a coach has lost some guys to other schools and started to panic. He's thinking, "Man, we've got to get this kid in. Let's try to get him to say yes in the next couple days." So he'll give this ultimatum.

To be clear, I'm not saying this is a dirty tactic by coaches, or that if a coach uses this tactic, he's a "bad" coach. It's recruiting. As a coach, you want to apply a little bit of pressure just to get a kid to make a decision, so you can either lock him up or move on.

Because the thing with recruiting is, sometimes the waiting is the hardest part (just like Tom Petty said). If a coach tells you, "Take a month and decide," and then a month goes by and you say no, now that coach has wasted a month. And now he can't go out and get other guys because they've already committed to other schools.

Likewise, if a coach tells you, "We want you, but I can't offer you anything just yet. Give me some time." And a month goes by, and then he says, "I don't have a scholarship for you," now *you've* wasted a month. And lesser players than you have accepted scholarships to colleges you would have said yes to.

So ideally, both sides should be respectful of the others' time constraints. But as a player, you should also realize that the "deadline" that the coach sets up might not be the final, final, final deadline. If a coach says, "Let me know within three days or the scholarship's off the table," and you come back five days later, you might be amazed how that scholarship offer has managed to stay just on the edge of that table.

If You Hear This...

"We're full at your position right now. If anything opens up, I'll let you know as soon as possible."

It Means...

"Have a nice life." Seriously – 99 percent chance you'll never hear from him again.

If You Hear This...

"At this time I'd like to offer you a full scholarship to play basketball here. You can say yes right now, or you can take a couple of days to think about it."

It Means...

"We like you. We really like you. And we want you to play for us. We really, really want you to play for us. Please sign."

If You Hear This...

"I just don't think this is the right spot."

It Means...

"Stop talking to me. Get out of my office and don't even use the bathroom in the building. No, I won't validate your parking."

If You Hear This...

"I've got two spots left. I want to sign one more big, maybe two. But I might end up signing one more guard like you. So I can't offer you anything today, but that could change."

It Means...

"You're 5-10 and I need someone 6-5. But I might end up taking the best available player I can find. Which might be you and it might not. So you should definitely keep your options open. And don't hold your breath waiting to hear back from me."

If You Hear This...

"I don't have a scholarship for you right now."

It Means...

"And I probably won't have one a month or a year from now either. Unless you can get your 6-10 teammate to change his commitment from UConn to here. Then yeah, we could probably find a scholarship for you."

If You Hear This...

"What's the most important thing that is going to help you make your decision?"

It Means...

"Tell me what will be the deciding factor for you so that I can tell you why we are the best option for you in that area."

If You Hear This...

"Who is going to help you make your college decision?"

It Means...

"Tell me who you're going to listen to the most, so I can start recruiting them and so I don't have to waste a lot of time on those people around you who you're not going to listen to anyway."

If You Hear This...

"We can only pay for your books."

It Means...

"I want you, but I don't want to have to give up anything to get you. And I won't lose sleep if you go somewhere else."

If You Hear This...

"You're out of district, but I can get you a scholarship to pay in-district tuition fees."

It Means...

"I see you as a good practice player. And you could possibly play, if the backup gets hurt."

If You Hear This...

"This half-scholarship is all I have left."

It Means...

"I want you here, but really, if you don't want to come here I won't be heart-broken. Oh, also, I might be lying. I might have one-and-a-half scholar-ships left. I just think I can get you for a half."

If You Hear This...

"You are still on a list of possibilities. I want to stay in touch and see what happens."

It Means...

"Feel free to buy a ticket and come watch our team play next year."

If You Hear This...

"You're still on my radar. You never know."

It Means...

"Actually, I do know. You're not in our plans."

If You Hear This...

"I'll call you."

It Means...

"I might call you."

If You Hear This...

"Oh, you've decided to decline our scholarship offer and sign with another school? Well, let me know if I can ever help you."

It Means...

"If it doesn't work out there, you can probably transfer here."

CHAPTER NINETEEN

A Few Other Rules of Thumb...

Here are some other common recruiting situations, and what they mean.

>>When an assistant coach calls or texts you once and you don't hear from him again, that means that you're on their list but they're not really interested. You should pursue other recruiting options.

>>If an assistant coach is calling or texting you consistently, but you've never heard from the head coach, that means they're keeping in touch with you and building a relationship with you in case the guys who are ahead of you fall through. Doesn't mean it won't work out here or you won't eventually get a scholarship offer, but you should keep your recruiting open.

>>If the head coach has called or texted you a few times and the assistant coach is calling and/or texting you a lot, that means you're probably at the top of their list. They're high on you; they really like you.

And a Few Other Things...

>>The faster coaches are to get back to you, the more interested they are in you. If they get back within 10 minutes to your call or text, they like you. If they get back five days later, they're not that into you.

>>Likewise, the faster you respond to coaches and the more you contact them, the more they'll assume you're interested. If you get back to them

within 10 minutes, they'll assume you like them. If you get back to them five days later or not at all, they'll assume you're not interested.

>>If a coach used to contact you a lot as a sophomore but now that you're a senior he doesn't, he's lost interest in you. Similarly, if a coach used to get back to you right away but now he doesn't, he's lost interest in you. (Unless you happen to be in a recruiting "dead period," when coaches can't contact recruits.)

>>If a coach used to call or text you once a month but now he calls or texts you once a week, he's gotten more interested in you. If he used to take five days to get back to you but now he takes 10 minutes, same thing – he's gotten more interested in you.

Now, a lot of these rules may seem obvious. But sometimes when you're caught up in the recruiting process and you really want a certain result to happen, you can be blind to the obvious. That's why it's often important to remove your emotion for a second and take a critical look at what's going on. It doesn't matter how bad you might want a certain school to "like" you, if it's not showing you much interest, the best thing for you to do is probably to move on and focus on other schools.

The truth can sometimes hurt, but it'll hurt less if you accept it early, when you've still got other options.

CHAPTER TWENTY

North Carolina, South Carolina or Coastal Carolina: Finding the Right Fit

OK. The coaches have stepped into your living room. They've sampled your mother's meatloaf. They've brought you to campus, made their pitches and slapped your picture on the cover of a fake sports magazine. Or maybe they haven't done any of that. But the main thing is, they've offered you scholarships. Big, beautiful athletic scholarships to play basketball at their schools.

First of all, congrats. Not a large percentage of high school basketball players make it to this step. Second of all: assuming you've got all the information you need on these schools, it's time to make an important decision about your future. It's time to decide on a college. Here are the nine key factors to consider, in my opinion, in order to choose the right school for you.

1. Coaching Staff

Make sure you have a good feel for the head coach and his assistants. Find out how long they've been at the school, where they were before this and what "coaching tree" they are a part of. In other words, who did they coach under, who was their mentor, and have assistant coaches who used to work under them gone on to become head coaches? That will give you some insight into the quality of coaching that they do.

Also, as we've talked about before, make sure you have a good feel for the system that they run, and whether it plays to your strengths. And be sure to look at how the coaching staff develops players – what recent players have gone on to play either in the pros or, if it's a JUCO, four-year D1 and D2 schools.

2. Teammates

On your campus visit, you'll want to grab the current players' phone numbers and communicate with them, post-visit. Because if you can get along with the current players and text with them and build a relationship with them, then they are probably pretty good teammates. And when you've got good teammates, that leads to good team chemistry, lots of wins and really great, unforgettable times. If you don't like the current players, well, then that's going to be a problem when you get to campus. Because now you're teammates with them.

When looking at future teammates, it's going to be mainly a gut reaction thing. It's not like there is a perfect way to choose teammates. But when you're deciding between two schools, you're probably going to have a pretty good idea about which group you like more.

The other thing, as mentioned before, is to take a hard look at which guys are playing your position, and what years they are. Now, you need to be competitive and confident in your abilities, and know that wherever you go you're going to have to fight for playing time. And you don't want to decide *not* to go to a school just because some kid's already there playing your position, and he's pretty good (because that would eliminate almost every school). Ideally, you want to feel like you can beat out anybody else for a spot, and coaches certainly want guys who think like that.

But, on the other hand, you should also be realistic. If you're a point guard, and the team has already signed another point guard who's a McDonald's All-American, or their current point guard is All-Conference and only a freshman (with no plans of jumping early for the pros), you might want to pick another school. There's a fine line between defeatism and realism.

3. Academics

Kind of broad, and it depends on your goals. If you're completely focused on becoming a pro basketball player, then maybe academics don't mean as much to you. On the other hand, if you're looking at a college basketball scholarship as a means to receiving a top-notch college education that will prepare you for a successful career outside basketball, then the academics aspect at a particular school will be very important (more important, even, than the basketball side). In that case, you might want to choose the school that has the better reputation for whatever program it is you'd like to study (like, say, engineering… or veterinary medicine… or costume design).

But in general, you'll want to make sure the school has the degree that you're looking for, and a strong academic support system in place for student-athletes. You might not need to pick a school that has a top 5 engineering program, but you'll want to make sure the school is accredited (whatever that means) and that it's going to help you move on to a job or a professional degree. And if you're deciding between two schools and everything else seems to be equal, you might as well go with the one with the better academics (like, say, Vanderbilt over Mississippi State).

4. Scholarships

If you've got a few scholarship offers, make sure you know how much each one covers. Are they all full scholarships? Are they all half scholarships? Do they vary? Do you get to keep your Pell Grant at one (if you qualify), whereas you don't at the others? Figure out how much you'll have to pay out of your own pocket at each school – most colleges list the estimated cost of attendance on their website – and decide how much that means to you. If money is really an issue, and one school is willing to cover everything and the other schools aren't, that might be your decision right there.

Again, remember the golden question to ask coaches is, "What will I be responsible for paying myself?"

Also remember: only you can decide what is the most important factor in your decision. Choosing a college is all about the right fit for you. You're probably going to have to give up something in some areas (that are less important to you) to find the right fit and make the best decision.

5. Housing

Not a huge factor, but something to consider. Where will you be staying? In a dorm? In a four-bedroom apartment? In a rickety little house with all the other players? How close is it to the practice facility/arena, and how close is it to campus? Does it come with furniture or no furniture?

Your housing is different from place to place, so it's worth asking about. It's also a financial issue. For example, if your scholarship covers room and board, and you live in a dorm (or other campus housing), you don't get a check. But if you're allowed to move off campus and share an apartment, you'll get a check to cover your room and board (based on cost of living in that city), and sometimes you'll have money left over.

6. Location

A more important factor than housing. Where is this place? What type of town is it in? Do you like the town? Could you see yourself living here? Does it make you feel comfortable? Does it excite you? Does it creep you out? Does it depress you? And how does it compare to the other colleges' locations? (In other words: what are your other options?) If the town is so small and crappy that you're always going to want to get the heck out of it, you might not want to go there. (Assuming you have other options.) Or if it's in such a tough environment that you don't feel safe, you might not want to go there either. These are all things to consider.

Something else to consider: do you want to go play in a big city, where there is lots to do, but you won't be the only show in town? Or do you want to play in a smaller city or a college town, where your school is the main attraction and your team is treated basically like the area's "pro" team? For example, Miami's a great city, but not a lot of people really care about the Miami basketball team. Conversely, Manhattan, Kansas, is not a bustling metropolis, but the townsfolk sure do like their Wildcats. So decide which scenario you prefer.*

*I'm biased, but my personal opinion is that it's better to be in a prototypical "college town," where the city is smaller, there aren't any major pro teams in the immediate area, and the college team gets treated like a big deal by its fans, who are passionate and loyal. In college towns, there's just a lot more interest in the team and how it's doing. Fans turn up in big numbers and cheer hard for you because, frankly, they've got nothing better to do. (Note: this also leads to more television time, because networks like to feature arenas that are rocking.) Miami is a cooler city than Manhattan, Kansas, no question about it. But how many people in Miami are going to care too much about the Hurricanes basketball team, when South Beach is right there – and LeBron and D-Wade are right there? Not many.

7. Proximity to Home

Related to location, how close is this college to your hometown, and how close do you *want* to be to your hometown? If your college is a couple hours or less from your home, your family and friends can come watch you play. On the other hand, if you're from New Jersey and playing college basketball at Arizona, your mom may only see one game of yours per season live (if any). You okay with that? You going to be homesick? (Every year, there's always one guy on every team who gets homesick. Is that going to be you?)

Another factor: how's the climate? Is it similar to your hometown's, or is it totally different? And again, you okay with that? If you hate cold weather, you might not want to leave Louisiana to go play at Wisconsin. (The counter argument to that would be: the basketball program and coaching staff are much more important than the weather. You can always man up and buy a coat.)

Another possible factor: is the location compatible with a career aspiration of yours? If you want to study marine biology, you might want to play at South Florida rather than Butler. If you want to one day own a winery, you'll probably want to go with Fresno State over Idaho. If you want to be an actor, go to UCLA, not Arkansas. If you want to major in hotel and restaurant management, go to... any school in the country.

8. Facilities and Equipment

How's the practice gym? (Is it booked around the clock with volleyball and women's basketball, or is it normally available? Do you need a coach to get in, or can you enter with a passcode 24 hours a day?) How's the arena? (What's the atmosphere like? Are the fans crazy? Is it loud?) How's the weight room? How's the student lounge? (Are there couches and a big flat-screen and a refrigerator and computers, or is there one shabby sofa and a 13-inch TV?) Also: do you care about this stuff?

At the lower-end schools, are your shoes paid for? Do you get practice gear? Do you have to pay for your own socks, compression shorts, jock straps, undershirts, wrist bands, head bands, elbow sleeves, calf sleeves – and how important is all that crap to you, if at all? At the big schools you get any-thing and everything under the sun, gear-wise. At smaller schools, you often have to pay for it yourself.

Speaking of gear – and the makers of gear – there's something else to be aware of. If your AAU coach happens to be steering you toward one school in particu-lar, make sure it's for the right reasons. He might be pushing you to that school because it's sponsored by the same athletic company as his AAU team (and he'd like to keep his sponsor happy), not because it's necessarily the best fit for you. Might be the right school for you anyway, but it's just something to keep in mind.

9. The Experience

All of those factors add up to the overall experience. Try to project in your mind how that's going to be. Do you see your next two to four years there being a great experience? This one's more of a gut thing. Close your eyes and picture yourself on that team, at that school, in that town. You getting excited? Do you see yourself succeeding? Growing? Working hard? Having the experience of a lifetime? And ultimately: what is your heart telling you? What is your gut telling you? Those two things are almost never wrong.

To Sum Up

Choosing your college – whether you're a basketball player or not – is a crucial decision. There's just no way around this fact. Choose wisely and you could set yourself up with the friends, skills and connections that will lead to a great career and a fun, satisfying life. Choose poorly and you could wind up with a frustrating college experience and a lifetime sprinkled with disappointment and regret.

But keep this in mind: sometimes there's more than one right decision. Sometimes there are two right decisions. Sometimes there are three right decisions. You could go to school A and do well. You could go to school B and do well. You could go to school C and do well. Sometimes you're choosing between three great options. And in that case, you can't go wrong. So just go with your gut and pick one.

Secondly: it's what you do after making a decision that will really dictate whether your experience is a successful one or not. If you go to a great situation but you don't work your butt off, you're not going to have a satisfying four years. Conversely, if you go to a so-so situation but you dive in head first, give it everything you've got and commit 100 percent to the team, you're going to have a good experience. Think of it like this: Michael Jordan didn't always make the best decision with the ball. But he made sure he made the most of whatever decision he *did* make. You should strive to do the same. Whatever college you choose, do everything you can to make it a good decision. Own your choice.

And If You're Still Having Trouble Deciding...

Ask yourself: what is my ultimate goal? Is it to play pro basketball? Is it to be part of a team that goes to the Big Dance? That goes to a Final Four? Is it to be in practices with a great coach, so that you can one day coach yourself? Is it to guard future NBA players in practice? Is it to be THE MAN at a college, no matter how low that level is? Is it to play 38 minutes per game, no matter how few people are in the stands? Is it to get a scholarship to a great school so that you can get an awesome education that will set you up for a lucrative 40-year career? Figuring out the one thing that you really want will help make the right choice more apparent to you.

To say it another way: once you figure out that one thing that you really want, the process of choosing a college should be a lot easier.

CHAPTER TWENTY-ONE

Final Thoughts

As I write this, it's late February of 2012. Jeremy Lin is causing a frenzy in the NBA. He's averaging 21 points and 8 assists a game for the month for the New York Knicks. This is a guy who wasn't offered a single college scholarship coming out of high school, not even from the college in his hometown – Stanford – which could have watched most of his high school career in person.

Think about that: Stanford assistants no doubt attended some of Lin's basketball games (to scout other players, if nothing else), watched the guy score 15 points and dish out 7 assists per game his senior year, lead his team to a 32-1 record and a state championship over national powerhouse Mater Dei, and still thought, "Nah, guy's not up to our level. Kid can't play. Not worth a scholarship. Pass."

The point being: coaches miss on guys. (Especially when kids don't look or play a certain way.) It's not that they've got something against you. It's just that they're guessing, based on what they believe and what they think they know. But in reality, they don't *know* anything. Not for sure. And as Jeremy Lin proved, a hundred coaches' trash might be one coach's treasure. (Lin went to Harvard and was All-Ivy League First Team his junior and senior years. Then he went to the NBA, where he's now packing stadiums and making millions.)

So if you're not getting any attention from college coaches, don't think that automatically means you can't play in college. Don't think that means there's not a place for you. You don't have to convince everybody. All you have to do is keep playing, keep believing and keep getting better (and eventually *someone* will notice). Chances are, if you're determined to play basketball in college, there's a place for you somewhere.

As we've talked about throughout this book, there are lots of colleges out there. Hundreds. And if you're good enough in college, even at a small college, pro scouts will find you. So don't give up the game you love just because you're not getting as many letters, phone calls and texts – or *any* of those things – as other guys seem to be getting. None of those coaches' opinions matter as much as your own opinion, and your own belief. It's like Abraham Lincoln said: "Always bear in mind that your own resolution to succeed is more important than any one thing." And it's like Woody Allen said: "90 percent of success is showing up." (Woody Allen: basketball fan.)

So if you want to keep playing after high school, then the solution is simple: keep playing after high school. (Use the tools we talked about in this book to do that.) Keep showing up. Keep trying out. Keep working on your game. Make them drag you off the court. Seriously. *Make them drag you off the court.*

Now, that's enough reading. Go outside and shoot some hoops.

ACKNOWLEDGEMENTS

Nate Mast would like to thank his parents for always supporting every activity in which he wanted to participate, his brother for competing in every sport possible growing up, Lon Kruger for giving him a life-changing opportunity, Bill Self for allowing the opportunities to continue, Kyle Jarnagin for guiding him to become the man he wants to be, and his wife, Ashley, and kids, Nolan and Kendall, for the daily reminders of how great God is. Thank you, God. Also, thanks to Shawn Donnelly, who is all about endurance. And finally, some words to live by: success is defined in your daily habits. No matter what happens, you get to choose to be bitter or be better.

Shawn Donnelly would like to thank Steve Mazzucchi for reviewing an early version of this book and offering extremely helpful feedback. He'd also like to thank Kelly and Mason Dively for letting him stay with them while working on this book. Finally, he'd like to thank Nate Mast for answering all his questions (well, most of them) and Starbucks for creating the Pike Place Roast coffee.

ABOUT THE AUTHORS

Nate Mast is a former walk-on at the University of Illinois and the current Director of Basketball Operations at Southern Illinois University in Carbondale, Illinois. Previously, Mast was head men's basketball coach at Parkland College, an assistant coach at the University of Arkansas at Fort Smith and a basketball grad assistant at the University of Kansas. He has a bachelor's degree from the University of Illinois and a master's in architecture from the University of Kansas.

Shawn Donnelly is a writer and editor in Brooklyn, New York. He has written for Esquire.com, *Maxim*, *Men's Fitness*, *Muscle & Fitness*, MadeMan.com and *ESPN Rise*. He is a graduate of the University of Missouri School of Journalism.

Made in United States
Orlando, FL
12 July 2025

62905669R00085